WORLD OF LAUGHTER
The Motion Picture Comedy Short, 1910–1930

WORLD OF LAUGHTER

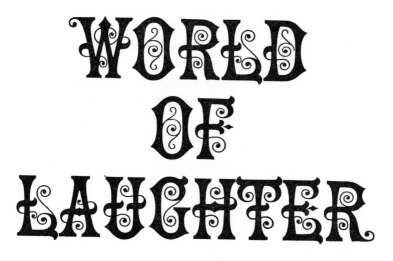

The Motion Picture Comedy Short, 1910-1930

Kalton C. Lahue

UNIVERSITY OF OKLAHOMA PRESS : NORMAN

BY KALTON C. LAHUE

Continued Next Week: A History of the Moving Picture Serial
(Norman, 1964)

World of Laughter: The Motion Picture Comedy Short, 1910–1930
(Norman, 1966)

LIBRARY OF CONGRESS CATALOG CARD NUMBER: 66–10292

Copyright 1966 by the University of Oklahoma Press, Publishing Division of the University. Composed and printed at Norman, Oklahoma, U.S.A., by the University of Oklahoma Press. First edition.

To my friend E. Mason Hopper
and
To my father Kenneth K. Lahue
Their love
of the motion picture comedy
made this book possible

ACKNOWLEDGMENTS

ONE of the most pleasant moments in putting the finishing touches on a volume involving copious research comes when the author stops to thank those who have assisted in his work. Few books are really the product of one man's efforts. Most authors owe a good deal more than they admit to friends, acquaintances, and associates. This particular book came about as the result of an idea of mine which Kent D. Eastin hammered into a concrete proposal one warm July afternoon in 1964. The proposal was accepted by my publishers a few weeks later, and special thanks go to them for their faith in my work.

The Academy of Motion Picture Arts and Sciences, the New York Public Library, and the Film Library of the Museum of Modern Art were all generous in providing the raw material from which film histories are made. The materials found in the San Joaquin County Library, Stockton, California, and the Lodi Public Library, Lodi, California, were also of great help. Mrs. William Horsley, Norman Taurog, E. Mason Hopper, Chester Conklin, Frank Leon Smith, William Campbell, and Fred New-meyer all gave generously of their memories. Samuel K. Rubin, Nick Fiorentino, Chris Collier, and Robert Cooper also contributed many ideas—as well as support and enthusiasm—which helped open the doors to many film collections for the purpose of refreshing my memory. To all those individuals who lent me films, many thanks. John Hampton, of the Silent Movie Theater in Los Angeles, was kind enough to schedule his programs to my convenience. I am especially indebted to those who made this book financially possible, and to my former editor Herbert H. Hyde, now of the University of Nebraska Press.

KALTON C. LAHUE

Mountain View, California
January 20, 1966

INTRODUCTION

Tʜɪs book deals with the men and companies who made laughter standard fare in the motion picture theaters of yesterday. It is a history of the silent motion picture short rather than a treatment of the nature of comedy, which has been a subject of discussion, even of controversy, for generations. It would be well, however, before attempting to show the evolution of silent comedy through the activities of those who were involved in its creation, to consider briefly the theory of comedy as it applies to the silent screen.

Comedy has been an element of human existence since the beginning of time, and every age has had its celebrated comics. And while we may often wonder what gave them their appeal when we read or see their work today, we must remember that their humor was as valid for its time and for the society in which they lived as ours is. They and their contemporaries shared a culture and an environment—they had something in common— just as we have something in common with our own comedy artists.

All silent screen comedy stems from the reaction of an individual to things in his environment. If the reaction of the comic induces an audience to laugh, he has accomplished his task. When we chuckle at an incident that occurs on a screen in front of us, we are amused at the composite picture of the individual, his environment, and his reactions. On the other hand, when all we see is a person in a foolish or ludicrous costume and still we laugh, the reaction is more our own, and the image on the screen is within our environment.

By virtue of its nature, silent screen comedy usually employs the law of contrasts. We laugh as the little man outwits the larger one, as the poor man gains an advantage over the wealthy man, and as the shy, ugly fellow triumphs over the handsome dandy. It is this law which establishes many comic situations, for we see any situation in terms of the people involved.

The greatest comedians in terms of impact on the public have been those working in an essentially visual medium, such as the motion picture. This can be easily explained, for such a mass medium is readily available to rich and poor alike. And because a visual experience is the most nearly universal in understanding and appeal, language is no barrier—a fall is a fall and a chase is a chase. No comedian in history, for example, has ever received anything equaling the exposure which movies have given to Charles Chaplin over the past fifty years.

Occasionally, we find persons who try to impart to the arts obscure theories of symbolic significance. The English professor who attempts to read an obscure meaning into a book which has become a classic is one example. No doubt many authors would be greatly surprised at some of the interpretations given their writings. I am not suggesting that such meanings could not or do not exist. I simply wish to remind the reader that the fact is too often overlooked that an author likely wrote his work as a response to a pressing need—money. In the same way, misguided but well-meaning social critics often lean over backward in an effort to attach deep and significant meaning to comedy. Film comedians have created works of enduring value, but an awareness of social significance on the part of the comic, his director, or his producer has rarely been the major motive. Generally, the idea of entertainment delivered for the dollar received lay back of their efforts.

Naturally, some screen comedians have been better received than others. Many have not stood the test of time, and when we view the samples of their work that are available today, we wonder where the humor went. We tend to forget that most comedy is contemporary and spontaneous in origin, having meaning and rendering humor only in terms of a specific environment or circumstance. A small handful of comedians rose above this narrow vision and created comedy on film which will never be dated. The majority of laugh-makers, however, were not as talented or as fortunate in their efforts. To bring this home forcefully to the reader, I ask him to consider how much of the verbal humor of our "sick" comics of today will be meaningful for future generations? I do not mean to say that their brand of humor does not have entertainment value for an audience of today. I only wish to point out that their humor for the most part is contemporary and depends upon the circumstances of our society.

Although many of the screen comedians who were immensely popular in their day have become obscure, their comic routines are no less funny today, but one must make an effort to understand their relationship to their audience. For example, pure slapstick, which makes use of knockabout comedy and in effect assaults the dignity of an institution, individual, or organization, was the chief ingredient of silent screen comedy. Laughter, the desired result of comedy, is directly related to society. We laugh at the policeman who gets hit in the face with a pie. The situation becomes even funnier if we know that a tramp trying to steal the pie delivered the *coup de grâce*. But we would not laugh as long or as hard if two tramps stood and threw pies at each other. Why? When an individual representing an institution has been the recipient of the pie, it reminds us that policemen are only human after all. The effect is to reduce the higher authority to a level that makes us feel equal or superior to it.

During Prohibition, many films portrayed drunks and drinking, a subject then very popular with audiences. To many viewers today, accustomed to taking a drink if or when they want one, such comedy lacks entertainment. Indeed, it may even be a bit offensive. Drinking is condoned, but the drunk is not. In context with its time, the film that poked fun at an unpopular law directly involved the audience of the day. We cannot fully appreciate or understand the mood of the times that made drunks and drinking comic subjects.

It should also be noted that the comedian, represented at the outset as a normal, average human, draws our laughter in quantity when he reacts in a bewildered but self-assured manner

xii

to the events in his environment. Why? Simply because we identify with him at the beginning. As it becomes apparent that he
does not quite understand what is going on around him, we
begin to feel superior, for who, we wonder, could be that stupid?
To repeat, successful comedy often gives the audience this feeling of superiority.

I have chosen the year 1910 to begin this narrative for several reasons. The available films made prior to this date are too
limited for review. The form of comedy shorts did not really
begin to mature until around 1910, and documentation of the
years before is scanty and highly unreliable. Some readers will
note the omission of the Biograph Company and will wonder
why more attention was not paid to such a creative organization. Biograph certainly made some interesting comedies during
1908–1909 and provided many future screen personalities with
a sound background for later success. However, it is my contention (and this will be argued by some) that the Biograph of
1910–13 was really the Biograph of D. W. Griffith. By 1913, the
firm was quite ill and would shortly succumb. I have also omitted
the films of Méliès in this consideration of comedy, for although
they were popular, they were French in origin, and by 1910
Méliès had abandoned his early techniques in a futile imitation
of American producers.

This is not a definitive history of the American comedy short.
No such work exists and it is doubtful that one ever will. The
problems involved in such an endeavor are beyond solution. The
major trade papers of 1913 list more than ten thousand reels of
film released for the year. Of these, approximately three thousand could be classified as comedies. A very rough estimate of
the number of comedy shorts produced in the silent film period
would probably give a total of more than forty thousand reels,
the vast majority of which are no longer available for viewing.

The number of film companies in these early days is fantastic, and material for documentation of the greater part of them has disappeared; thus the task of providing a comprehensive history is insurmountable.

I have dealt with feature comedy to some extent, especially as it has figured in the later careers of comedians whose humble beginnings were in short subjects. It is impossible to consider the genius of a Chaplin and a Keaton without also examining their longer feature comedies. This further explains the absence of Douglas Fairbanks, Douglas MacLean, and many others whose light comedies were well received in the twenties. Their work needs different treatment and deserves a volume of its own. This book belongs to those screen comics whose mainstay was the short subject.

I have thus placed certain limits on the contents to follow and have settled for what I hope is a representative sampling of films, firms, and people. In being selective, I have attempted to choose—within the bounds of the documentary materials available—those which I felt would provide a well-rounded picture. Let us now concentrate on the funmakers whose antics are still fondly recalled by a generation which laughed at them daily, not so very long ago.

ILLUSTRATIONS

WORLD OF LAUGHTER
The Motion Picture Comedy Short, 1910–1930

CHAPTER ONE

The American Comedy, 1910–13

I N 1910 the American silent mo-
tion picture comedy was in a sorry state. In the first place, not
enough domestic comedy films were being produced to satisfy
the demand. Of the twenty-eight licensed releases for the week
of February 26, 1910, only six—or 21 per cent—were comedies.
Twenty were dramas, and the remaining two comprised one
industrial and one scenic reel. These releases seem to be sufficient, but this was the period in cinema history when the single
reel was the dominant length for exhibition, and programs had
to be changed very frequently.

On January 30, 1910, the Film Service Association, a representative group of exhibitors, met in New York City and went on record as being sharply opposed to any reel over nine hundred feet in length. It was their considered opinion that twelve minutes was the longest span of time any patron cared to devote to a single topic. They also condemned the companies which put together a 1,000-foot reel consisting of a main subject of 850 to 875 feet, to which a short comedy of 100 to 125 feet was then added. Most of the members of the association did not bother to exhibit the latter, cutting it off instead.

With this characteristic exhibitor attitude in mind, what were the circumstances surrounding the comedy film? For the most part, comedies were of the split-reel variety, ranging from three to four hundred feet in length. Some were even shorter, like the Edison release, *The New Policeman* (December, 1909), a mere one hundred feet in length. Although the dramatic offerings were not much longer, it had become recognized by this time that to try to tell a story in less than five hundred feet was impossible. Thus the comedy was relegated to being a "filler," for it was easy to film a short chase prompted by a ridiculous reason or to show a few humorous happenings.

A fine example of this sort of film was the Vitagraph release, *The Beautiful Snow* (March, 1910), in which a father peered out of his window one morning and discovered that a heavy snowfall had taken place during the night. Stepping out of the house to take a brisk walk, he fell down the slippery stairs. From this ludicrous beginning, it was the father's eventual misfortune to be caught in the middle of a snowball fight, to get hit by some boys sliding down a hill, and to have snow poured down his neck, courtesy of a group of urchins leaning out of a window above him. At this point, the father hastily withdrew to a store

4

front where he hoped to warm up, and was greeted by the proprietor, who promptly let down the awning and buried poor father in snow as the 426-foot reel faded out.

Surprisingly, Vitagraph gained an early reputation as a leader in the field of comedy-drama, one we will examine at greater length later. Biograph and Imp also shared this distinction for a short time. In the field of straight comedy, Essanay and Lubin tied for honors during 1910–13. The firms actively interested in decent comic offerings were trying hard to acquire an aura of respectability for their product. Vitagraph advertised all of its releases with high-sounding phrases. Its release of *A Pair of Schemers* (January, 1910) was accompanied by the information that it was a "high class comedy with a novel ending. Neat and classy."

Helping to fill the demand for laugh-provoking films, several foreign producers did a lucrative business in the United States at this time. Gaumont, Urban, Lux, and The Great Northern Film Company released weekly offerings. The output of the New York Motion Picture Company included one reel each week by Ambrosio and Itala, two Italian firms.

As if it were not enough that quantity was sadly lacking, so too was quality. Many of the better early comedies came from France, where producers seemed to exercise more imagination in their work. Even though comedy must be viewed in relation to the environment which produced it, a large number of the 1910–11 American releases simply were not funny—then or now. Many were merely aimless slapstick of the lowest type.

One may wonder today, as did the literate audiences of yesterday, why so many films used ridiculous themes. Two of the most overworked situations were a mother handing her baby to a stranger to care for while she shopped, and a father entrusting his child to an obvious bum while he enjoyed the pleasures of a neighborhood saloon. The comedy stemmed from the mishaps which the erstwhile guardian suffered.

Comedy based on an improbability is good farce if handled correctly, but farce has to be possible in order to be funny, and the breakdown in these two themes came at the very outset. The success of such films can be credited to two facts: the audiences were undiscriminating, and the frequent changes of program created an almost insatiable demand for films—any films that would entertain.

The comedy of this period was also daring and risqué, even by today's liberal standards. It is a shame that a print of *A Queen of the Burlesque,* an Edison release of February 11, 1910, is not available for viewing today. A review in *The Moving Picture World* advised the exhibitor in this manner: "A picture based upon a development of extravagant humor which can scarcely be described in print. But perhaps it is sufficient to say that some mischief-loving children, bent upon vengeance, succeeded in making a spinster very ridiculous in the eyes of an elder of the church and he breaks off the engagement. It is all extravagantly funny and causes more than one laugh even though there is a species of broad suggestion which may be resented by some, or, at least, deplored. . . . Better look at the picture and make your own decision."[1] As the entire film lasted only a bit over four minutes, there was little time for development of this plot along other than hasty and broad lines.

Essanay released *The Latest in Garters* (April, 1910), a 525-foot offering which dealt with feminine garters, adorned with bells. A group of boys who were determined to see the garters in use introduced mice as the means of causing the girls to disclose

[1] *The Moving Picture World,* February 26, 1910, p. 298.

6

the source of the tinkling music, and succeeded in raising audience eyebrows at the same time.

The plight of the comedy short did not improve greatly during 1911. The majority of releases were stereotypes, primitive in nature, that often resorted to simple buffoonery in incoherent chases rather than developing any genuine comic interest. Considering both the licensed and the independent releases, by the end of 1911 the production of dramas outnumbered that of comedies by about sixteen to one. Comedies were just not anyone's forte at this time.

An interesting fact, seldom recalled today, was the number of westerns that were being made. By the close of 1911, at least one-third of all releases were westerns. Many dealt with the American Indian, and successful pictures about the life of the red man were made not only here, but abroad. In the United States, Kalem was a leading producer of such films, having the services of Red Wing and Mona Darkfeather. Actually, Kalem concentrated on westerns, along with historical reels such as *Railroad Raiders of '62,* a 1911 version of the Andrews Raid during the Civil War. So many Indian pictures, in fact, good and bad, were made that several tribes registered a protest against them with the Bureau of Indian Affairs in Washington. Government officials met each tribal delegation with a firm promise to inform the offending companies of the objections, but the films continued to flood the screen.

Many exhibitors began to cry out for more and better comedies as the year 1911 ended. The response was negative. Few producing firms felt that they could achieve a sound financial position from comedies alone, and those few that did acknowledge the need were not about to undertake the task for fear of becoming martyrs. They realized that drama kept them solvent.

It was not until the advent of Keystone in August, 1912, that a single firm devoted its total output to humor and prospered in the doing.

With E. V. Townsend writing the scripts, Edison had released a number of comedies during 1910, few of which were notable. The only real success was a series of split-reel offerings starring "Bumptious," a fat little man who was quite impressed by his own importance. An actor, identified only as "Jonesy," began this series with the first release in June, 1910. During 1911, Edison sharply curtailed its production of comedies, concentrating instead on history and drama.

Pathé which was producing its films in France at this time, released a subject as timely today as it was in April, 1911. *The Trading Stamp Mania* told the story of an unfortunate man whose wife had been bitten by the desire to paste stamps into the books. Exaggerated for comedy effect, it was nonetheless an interesting commentary on its day, for even some of the theaters gave trading stamps to their patrons in 1911.

The trade papers also raised a loud voice in support of exhibitors for more and better comedies in 1911. As there can be only so many variations on one theme, skillful construction became necessary to assure decent and humorous results. George Rockhill Craw, an early critic and writer for *The Moving Picture World*, outlined his theory for the production of well-conceived comedies. According to him comedies had to be "structured" in a manner similiar to the dramas of the day. He viewed each comedy as consisting of three parts or phases: (1) the introduction, (2) the middle or climax, and (3) the end or denouement.[2] Few took note of Craw's opinions.

A few weeks later, an article appeared in which a call was

[2] *The Moving Picture World,* January 28, 1911, pp. 178–79.

8

made for specialization on the part of producers.[3] Many men directed a drama followed by a comedy and then another drama. It was the contention of *The Moving Picture World* that few directors could successfully switch gears that rapidly. The magazine also pointed out that comedy was a fine art and, as such, required certain talents not available to the average director. It was further suggested that men who possessed the comic touch should work in that field only and that higher prices should be offered and paid for comical scenarios, the writing of which was also an art.

One of the greatest difficulties in writing a comedy scenario was preserving the action as straight comedy and at the same time keeping it above the level of farce or burlesque. The ideal one-reel comedy was one which progressed briskly and continuously from one amusing situation to another, directly toward the climax, yet managed to maintain suspense until the end of the reel. This ideal was by no means easy to achieve, for the haste with which production was accomplished left little time to alter or improve the final result.

Selig's films, which had received much favorable comment from early reviewers, were less successful during this period. High-quality laboratory work had given way to dark, muddy prints, and exhibitors canceled their orders in droves. Business had been so good for Selig in 1909 that the Chicago facilities were scheduled for expansion in 1910.

However, labor disputes held up completion of the work for nearly a year, and as the proper equipment to handle production was not available, the overworked lab turned out some rather poor work. By 1911, Selig was back in business in a big way. The completed facilities soon put an end to the exhibitors' complaints.

[3] *Ibid.*, April 8, 1911, p. 755.

In one manner of speaking, the American short comedy was to see astounding progress in 1912. Even though Vitagraph, Lubin, and Essanay had acquired the best reputations in the industry, they were to be quickly replaced by the Keystone madness of Mack Sennett. Within a year after its founding, Keystone would set the pace for others to follow.

The percentage of comedy releases did not increase measurably during the year. The licensed companies turned out fifty-three reels during the week of September 23–28, of which only sixteen could be classified as comedies. Not too surprisingly, the independent producers came very close to this figure, with fifty reels, of which only thirteen were comedies.

The year 1913 witnessed a huge expansion in the number of producing firms. Whereas in 1911 only seven units had been working in the Los Angeles area, by the end of 1912 thirty-five legitimate motion picture units were at work, with an estimated investment of $1,500,000. Many more were to come and go rapidly in the next two or three years. An example was the Graphic Film Company, which lasted one month. At the end of that time, a legal document was tacked on its door stating that pending settlement of a $74.00 claim, the property belonged to the sheriff. Anyone with a camera could go into the motion picture business at that time, but it took a good deal more to succeed. Although the General Film Company began releasing two-reel subjects to the exhibitors late in 1912, many comedies were still of the short or split-reel variety and would remain so until about the middle of 1915.

With an estimated fifteen thousand theaters actively exhibiting movies in 1912, the situation in regard to comedies was still unsatisfactory in both number and quality of productions. But a pattern of screen humor was emerging in the comedy shorts.

CHAPTER TWO

The Comedy of General Film

V ITAGRAPH was the most pro-
lific and important comedy producer in the General Film Company program.[1] Beginning in 1910 with John Bunny, it led in
the production of domestic and social comedies until the early
twenties. Earlier humorous films released by the firm had been
full of rowdy antics, much like the early comedies featuring J.

[1] General Film was the distributing company formed by the Motion Picture
Patents Company to handle the products of its members—Edison, Biograph,
Vitagraph, Lubin, Selig, Essanay, Pathé, Kalem, Méliès, and Kleine.

11

Stuart Blackton as Happy Hooligan.[2] By World War I, the best polite comedy bore the big "V" trademark and featured Bunny and the ever popular Mr. and Mrs. Sidney Drew.

The portly John Bunny was born in New York City on September 21, 1863, the son of a British naval officer who had emigrated to the United States. He grew up in Brooklyn, where for a while he worked as a clerk in a neighborhood market. This did not satisfy him, however, and Bunny ran away, becoming a roving player and end man in various obscure minstrel shows. Bunny eventually worked his way up to the legitimate stage, and during the 1897–98 season, he was the manager and director of the Grand Opera House in Salt Lake City. The following seven years were spent as stage manager and director for William A. Brady. In 1905–1906, Bunny toured in productions of *Easy Dawson;* in 1906–1907, *A Midsummer Night's Dream;* in 1907–1908, *Tom Jones;* and in 1908–1909, *Fluffy Ruffles.* He concluded his stage career in 1910 with an appearance in Lew Fields' production of *Old Dutch.*

By this time, Bunny was forty-seven and earning $150 weekly on the boards. Having carefully watched the growth of movies and nickelodeons, he decided that films could do something for him that the stage would never be able to accomplish: they could give him world fame. Consequently, he went down to the Flatbush studio of Vitagraph and inquired about employment. To convince a dubious Albert E. Smith, he offered to do a picture without pay—a film later identified by Smith in his autobiography, *Two Reels and a Crank,* as *Dr. Cupid.*[3]

Smith was struck by the expressive features of Bunny's face and the extravagant emotions they could convey. He was also

[2] Blackton was a co-founder of the film, along with Albert E. Smith and William T. Rock.

[3] No such title was released by Vitagraph in 1909–11. The nearest to it was *Cupid and the Motor Boat* in January, 1910.

impressed by Bunny's size and build, for the actor weighed about three hundred pounds—all contained in a short barrel-like body. Bunny was far from handsome, but he had a merry charm, and Vitagraph had made no mistake when he finally accepted the offer of $40.00 a week. Whether his new actor would stay in pictures or return to the stage, however, Smith could not be sure. For Bunny the decision was already made. He was an actor of the first caliber and he knew it. By 1913 his salary had risen to $1,000 a week, and he remained with Vitagraph until his death in 1915. Bunny never signed a formal contract; he believed that a handshake or a few words of agreement between gentlemen were sufficient.

His popularity with audiences was not to be doubted. When he went on a diet in 1912 and lost forty pounds, it caused consternation at the box office and he quickly regained his old form. Often teamed with the scrawny Flora Finch, a perfect foil for his shenanigans, he made more than two hundred comedies and a number of dramatic appearances before his death.

Miss Finch was in her own right a fine actress and as homely as Bunny. In the early days of screen comedy, no team was more appreciated than that of Bunny and Finch. They were among the earliest comedians to be billed by name, an accomplishment which came about partly because Bunny's name appeared in many of the titles of his films.

Bunny's popularity extended to every country where Vitagraph films were played. When he was sent abroad in May, 1912, to make a number of pictures based on Charles Dickens' *Pickwick Papers,* crowds plagued him wherever he went. This was enough proof to John that his decision to make movies had been a correct one. Working at the Hepworth studio with a group of English actors, he made *Bunny at the Derby* and three single-reel episodes from *Pickwick Papers* before returning home in September. These were later combined to make a three-reel film and were re-released as such.

Although these films proved that Bunny could do excellent dramatic work, they were not his most popular ones with audiences, who preferred his farce comedies. Much of Bunny's screen success came from his adeptness at making audiences cry one moment and laugh the next. His comedy style was a refined pantomime several cuts above the crude slapstick that characterized most comics of the time. Many of the plots of his films revolved around his immense size. He was also fond of disguising himself as a woman in his comedies, a feat which he carried off quite well. His films contained a great deal of flirting and extra-marital high jinks as well as drinking and smoking, but these were all handled with careful attention to good taste.

In *Her Hero* (September, 1911), he portrayed a timid husband who collapsed when a holdup he had staged for the benefit of his wife turned out to be the real thing. The aspiring politician who dreamed himself out of office but back into the good graces of the widow he loved was the subject of *The Politician's Dream* (November, 1911). In another picture, Bunny decided that his young daughter Helen needed a governess and so hired an ugly old maid (Flora Finch) with one redeeming feature— her long, beautiful hair, with which he fell promptly in love. To rid herself of his attentions, Flora was forced to cut *Her Crowning Glory* (September, 1911). Bunny played Santa Claus in *Ida's Christmas* (December, 1912), which also included Dolores Costello as a poor child who returned a purse which she had found and received a reward of money, a Christmas tree, and many other gifts for her honesty.

By the middle of 1912, Bunny and Miss Finch began to make somewhat regular screen appearances as man and wife, in which they were variously billed as Mr. and Mrs. Bunny, or Mr. and

Mrs. Brown. Regardless of the names of the leading characters, however, the fans referred to their pictures as "Bunnygraphs," "Bunnyfinches," or "Bunnyfinchgraphs."

One film had Bunny, cleaned out in an all-night poker game, arriving home to find Flora, the charming wife, waiting up for him. Promising to play no more poker, he retired to scheme a way out of his word. The opportunity came in the form of an invitation to join an exclusive club. As its meeting night was the same as that of his weekly poker game, Flora agreed that it was a fine idea for him to join. But Bunny confessed the truth later in his sleep, and Flora soon began plotting *A Cure for Pokeritis* (February, 1912). With the help of her cousin Freddie, who in turn enlisted the aid of his Bible class, Bunny was trailed and the deception confirmed. The following week, Freddie and his friends dressed up as policemen and raided the game. Meanwhile, Flora had rounded up the wives, and they all descended upon the erring husbands.

In *Stenographers Wanted* (February, 1912), Brown and Jones (Bunny and Charles Eldridge) each needed a new stenographer. A sign was hung out, and the office was soon filled with luscious girls. Both men inspected the applicants, and one chose a blonde (Lillian Walker), the other a brunette (Leah Baird). Unfortunately for the men, their wives (Kate Price and Julia Swayne Gordon) had already made their choice. Marching into the office, they took their husbands by the ear to show them a real bargain—Flora Finch, of course.

Bunny took a vacation in January, 1913, to make his first appearance in vaudeville. He was besieged with offers from all over the world, but after a few weeks of the strenuous life, he returned to the screen. One of his more famous comedies of this period was *The Autocrat of Flapjack Junction* (October, 1913). As the operator of a boardinghouse, he was desperate. The competition of Widow Finch was ruining his business. Toying with the idea of suicide, Bunny went into the forest where he accidentally rescued a group of chorus girls. They returned the favor by patronizing his boarding house, thus convincing the widow that she had no future in business. But Finch and Bunny ended the single-reel comedy by merging their operations and marrying. (It was also in 1913 that Bunny, as a publicity stunt, insured his face for $50,000 against the chance that his "beauty" would be lost.)

As a stern, determined father in *Love, Luck, and Gasoline* (May, 1914), he attempted to thwart the elopement of his tomboyish daughter (Lillian Walker). She was equally determined to marry an athletic young man (Wally Van), and the three-reel comedy ended with a chase involving a yacht, motor boats, and even airplanes. In *Love's Old Dream* (January, 1914), Flora Finch portrayed Miranda, an old maid intent upon outwitting her young and beautiful rival, played by Ethel Lloyd. They both had an eye for an elderly professor (Bunny), and Flora planted a camera in his study to photograph him in a moment of indiscretion which she was positive would take place. Her plot failed, for she was the person caught in the compromising position, and the two true lovers married.

Polishing Up (February, 1914), opened with Bunny giving Flora a hard time about her appearance in the morning. Making up, they locked arms to drink the breakfast coffee. Bunny returned to his room to dress while Flora did the same. She had decided to take a vacation. While the cat's away, the mouse will play, but poor Bunny was rebuffed in his first attempt to pick up a young girl. The second effort was better received—Bunny got picked up by two! While lunching with his new friends, Bunny was invited to visit them at a seaside hotel. He declined at first, but finally accepted.

Flora, in the meantime, had arrived at the seashore and signed into the hotel as Vivian Astor, where she was spotted by a young doctor who believed her to be wealthy. Flora sprained her ankle upstairs just as Bunny and the two girls registered downstairs. The girls soon met Flora and told her of the rich old gentleman who was in love with both of them. They discussed their amours and planned a get-together for all five. On the appointed night, Bunny and his wife came face to face, realized each other's indiscretions, and made up quickly. All sat down to the meal with Bunny's toast, "Here's to our wives and sweethearts—may they never meet!"

Bunny's career ended in the spring of 1915. He had wanted to go back on tour and had left Vitagraph in the summer of 1914 to prepare an around-the-world itinerary. His plans were disrupted by the outbreak of the war in Europe and he was forced to cancel the overseas portion of the trip, confining it to major American cities. Mobbed wherever he traveled, Bunny went all-out to make the tour a success. He returned home in April, 1915, where he died on the twenty-sixth, after a brief, two-weeks' illness, from a combination of Bright's disease and overexertion.[4]

Flora Finch was ruined when her partner died, although she didn't know it at the time. Vitagraph decided to star her in a series of her own with Jay Dwiggens and Templer Saxe. The series began and ended with *The Starring of Flora Finchurch* (May, 1915). In this gem, she played a country girl who inherited $5,000 and promptly dropped her country lover, Hiram. Starting out on a theatrical career, she lasted only as long as her money. Penniless and ridiculed by audiences, she was reclaimed

---

[4] In 1918, his brother George, not quite as stout as John, tried to succeed as a comedian for Goldwyn. His greatest asset was his resemblance to his famous brother, but it was not enough.

by Hiram in a happy ending. The film did not go over with the audiences, and Vitagraph relegated her to minor supporting roles for the next two years.

In 1917 she formed the Flora Finch Film Company, opening with *War Prides* (April), a two-reel travesty on the popular Nazimova feature, *War Brides*. The subtitles consisted mostly of a tedious series of painful puns. Flora's company turned out crude burlesque and poor slapstick, and her career plummeted into oblivion. Until her death in 1940, she played minor and extra roles whenever she could.

As if one oversized comic on the lot were not enough, Vitagraph hired Hugh McGowan in 1913. Terry Ramsaye claimed that McGowan (twenty-nine years old and 367 pounds) was a Brooklyn undertaker whom Smith and Blackton had discovered sleeping on a park bench. Remembering that Bunny was also a fat man who liked to doze on the set at times, they reasoned that another sleepy fat man might prove equally funny. Mc-Gowan changed his name to Hughie Mack and supported Bunny during 1913 in such films as *John Tobin's Sweetheart* (September, 1913). The scene was set by a shipwreck in the South Seas. Captured by natives and sentenced to death, Mack took advantage of an attack by a neighboring tribe and hilariously fought them off with his revolver. His reward was the hand of a native princess with whom he had fallen in love. Meanwhile, back in civilization, another man (Bunny) with the same name married Hughie's waiting fiancée.

Mack also starred by himself in farcial slapstick films during 1913–15. In *Roughing the Cub* (June, 1913), he was supported by Herb Barry and Harry Northrup. The story told of the misadventures of a fledgling reporter who was sent out on fake stories by his co-workers. In the end, of course, he scooped them all with the biggest story in the paper's history. In 1916, Mack starred with Patsy de Forest in his own series, written by Graham Baker and Larry Semon, but he failed to reach the degree of popularity which Bunny had gained. Mack was neither as polished an actor nor as funny as the man with whom he had once worked. His comic style was somewhat different and leaned to the light side of slapstick. This is understandable when it is considered that Semon, who was later to develop a comic following of his own, directed him as well as co-writing the scripts. Mack moved to Henry Lehrman's L-KO Company in August, 1917, and then joined Sennett at Paramount in 1919 before fading into obscurity in the twenties at Universal, where he provided comic relief for features and serials. On October 13, 1927, he was found dead in his Santa Monica apartment, victim of an apparent heart attack.

Almost as popular as Bunny and Finch, Mr. and Mrs. Sidney Drew utilized a slightly different approach in their comedy. Whereas Bunny was often portrayed as trying to escape the clutches of a shrewish female, the Drews most often projected themselves as an average married couple. They played upon the follies and foibles of married life to the delight of millions.

Drew, who was born on August 28, 1864, was a leading man for Charles Frohman on the legitimate stage before entering films. An uncle of the Barrymores, he was the half-brother of John Drew. His first wife and comedy partner on the stage, Gladys Rankin, also had a distinguished lineage (her parents were McKee Rankin and Kitty Blanchard) and was an accomplished writer under a pseudonym. Drew's first screen appearance for which he received billing was in September, 1911, in a Kalem release, *When Two Hearts Are Won.* This was one of his own stage sketches, filmed in one reel. As Kalem was not enthusiastic about comedies at the time, Drew moved to Vitagraph in 1913, where he played supporting roles opposite Anita Stewart, Dorothy Kelly, and John Bunny, among others.

Mrs. Drew was not well and died soon after. Within six months after her untimely death, Drew married Lucille McVey on July 25, 1914. Miss McVey worked in the scenario department at Vitagraph and sometimes acted under the name "Jane Morrow." She was to become Drew's partner in a team that turned out many memorable comedy films, some of which she wrote.

At the beginning of his starring career with Vitagraph, Drew often portrayed a character with problems, the source of most of them being a cantankerous uncle. In *Jerry's Uncle's Namesake* (January, 1914), he was spied by a reporter as he picked out presents for a neighbor's new baby. The reporter wrote an account of the shopping trip but mistakenly assumed that the gifts were for Jerry's baby. The published article reached his uncle (L. Rogers Lytton), who lived in the country, and the uncle wrote to Jerry, hinting at a big check in return for an invitation to visit.

Jerry and his wife (Louise Beaudet) borrowed a baby for the uncle's visit, but the baby's mother came and took it away shortly after the old gentleman first saw the child. Then Uncle decided that he wanted another peek at the baby, and pandemonium reigned when Jerry and his wife discovered the baby was gone. Both went out in search of another. Jerry returned first and showed the baby to Uncle, who exclaimed, "My God, twins?" In the meanwhile, the wife had located a third child and returned to show this one to an aghast uncle ("My God, triplets?") while Jerry was out of the room. Uncle, deciding that he was being hoodwinked, took back his check and stomped out, bringing the two-reeler to a close.

In another picture, Arthur (Drew) loved Dorothy, his uncle's ward. Unable to convince Uncle that he was fit to marry her, Arthur continued to see her and was rewarded for his diligence by being bodily thrown out of the house. Discouraged and disgusted, he wrote that it was all right because he had been married for a year anyway. When his uncle announced his intention of visiting the young couple, Arthur hastily produced a neighbor's wife as his own. Unable to keep away from Dorothy during the visit, he soon impressed uncle as being a potential bigamist, and the fun began in *Too Many Husbands* (June, 1914, two reels).

Drew, like Bunny before him, often built his comedies around the slightest of situations. In *Wanted, a Nurse* (January, 1915), he portrayed a wealthy young man who met a nurse after he was hurt in a trifling accident. In order to see her again, he pretended to be sick and thus won her. In *The Story of a Glove* (May, 1915), Mr. Huggins (Drew) left for a college reunion party. To remind him to come home early, his wife (Mrs. Drew, under her stage name Jane Morrow) put one of her gloves into his coat pocket. Naturally, Huggins did not notice it until he returned home, late as usual, and so was aghast when he discovered it in front of his wife. He recited an elaborate story (told in flashbacks) about the unfortunate incident that had placed it there. His wife listened patiently before revealing where it really came from, but unabashed, he persisted in his story.

Another typical Drew film was *A Safe Investment* (October, 1915). Charley Sharp (Drew) scolded his wife for not being able to manage her finances better. Unknown to her, he had established a crooked investment company and his advertisements soon began to pay off. Money came in so fast that he carried it home in baskets. Determined to show him how smart she really was, the wife meanwhile decided to make a killing in the stock market. As fast as he brought the money home, she took

21

it back and invested it in her husband's phony firm, not knowing that he was connected with the company. When the law
closed in and Charley headed home for the loot, he discovered
the terrible truth. Docile and unresisting, he pleasantly invited
the police to lock him away where he would be safe from his wife.

By October, 1915, a Mr. and Mrs. Sidney Drew comedy in
one or two reels was released every week. One of the classics
from this period was *Miss Sticky-Moufie-Kiss* (October, 1915).
The title comes from the nickname the husband gave his wife
after their marriage. Among her many assets, the wife spoke only
baby talk, loved her husband devotedly, and wished to be near
him constantly, which at first pleased him. It was not long, however, before the husband realized that she was not a wife, but
human flypaper—with his own poor self as the fly! Unable to
stand it any longer, he sadly put on his hat and coat and waded
out into the cold ocean until he disappeared.

In their films the Drews insisted on decency both in story
idea and thought and in characterization. Sidney Drew always
gave his wife credit for three-quarters of the story ideas and
wanted to share credit with all those to whom it was due.

Louis B. Mayer, eager to acquire a roster of proven performers for his newly founded Metro, made the Drews a better
offer than Vitagraph could or would match, and they moved to
Metro in January, 1916, at a joint salary of $90,000 a year. Vita-
graph reissued a series of its Bunny and Drew comedies in 1916
and again in 1918. At Metro, the Drews began a series of fifty-
two single reels yearly with *At the Count of Ten* (March, 1916)
and continued to turn out substantially the same type of films
they had made for Vitagraph.

The Hypochondriac (June, 1917) was a typical example. The
wife, Mrs. Brooks, was a woman who craved all the sympathy
and pity she could get. Continually ill, she finally declared that

if she knew her husband would have a second wife who would keep him happy, she could die peacefully. Sending for three of her most unattractive single friends, she presented them to him to choose from. The husband, in turn, presented a beautiful young girl whom he had hired as a maid and nurse for his wife. He devoted nearly all his attention to her and ignored his wife's choices. Waking up to reality, the wife soon recovered from all her illnesses, and they were "happy ever after."

At the end of 1918, the Drews left Metro to appear in a stage play in New York City, *Keep Her Smiling*. They also formed the VBK Corporation to produce their own comedies and made three before signing a contract with Paramount for release. This contract called for one comedy of two reels each month, a considerable cutback from the pace they had been keeping. Under this contract, *Romance and Rings* was the first production released; *A Sisterly Scheme,* the last film that Drew made prior to his death, was released in August, 1919. These were the same type of polite, social comedies which had made the duo famous.

Three things in life Drew held in the highest esteem (not necessarily in this order): his work, his son by his first wife, Sidney Rankin Drew, and liquor. Drew drank before and after work, on and off the set, but he despised drunks much in the same manner as W. C. Fields, another noted tippler, did. Drew invariably had several Manhattans after breakfast and before work. In the polite world of drawing-room comedy, cold tea was used as a substitute for liquor on the set. But when Drew was on the set, he took care that this nicety was surreptitiously disposed of and the decanter refilled with the real item. Supposedly an arrangement just between the property department and the star, it was actually an open secret on the set. Drew was able to consume an immense amount of liquor without showing

its effects, and Albert E. Smith once estimated that one decanter of whiskey would last the actor through a one-reel film
—providing there were no delays in shooting.

Drew's son began as an actor and then advanced to director
for Vitagraph, a seemingly promising career before him. The
young man was in love with actress Anita Stewart, but she did
not return his affection and married Rudy Cameron, her leading
man. Young Drew enlisted in the Lafayette Escadrille during
1917 and was killed in action just before the war ended. His
father, who had been ailing for some time, took the boy's death
very hard and died in early April, 1919.

After Drew's death, Mrs. Drew continued on the screen and
produced a short series of "After Thirty" stories with John Cum-
berland for Pathé. She died in 1926.

Throughout its history, Vitagraph released other comedy
series, and except for the films of Larry Semon, none proved to
be very successful with audiences. The Jarr Family series in
1915, from the Roy L. McCardell stories, was one example.
Directed by Harry Davenport, it starred Rose Tapley, Paul
Kelly, Frank Bunny, and Charles Eldridge.

Fred Karno's English music hall touring company, which had
brought Chaplin and Stan Laurel to America, graduated Jimmy
Aubrey to a series under the direction of Larry Semon, beginning with *Footlights and Fakers* (March, 1917). Aubrey came
to Vitagraph fresh from his success in the Starlight comedies
but stayed only a short time. He left in August to appear in the
Smallwood Film Company's comedies, co-directed by William
Seiter and C. Jay Williams. By 1919 he was back in the Vitagraph fold with a series that was well received by exhibitors.
Vitagraph's comedy team of Earl Montgomery and Joe Rock
were on their way out, and Larry Semon was carrying the Vitagraph program by himself. Aubrey was a welcome addition.

In February, 1914, debonair Billy Quirk joined Vitagraph. Once a great favorite in Biograph and Solax films, his career was now on the decline, but during 1914–16, he made a series of humorous one-reel comedies with Constance Talmadge and others under the Vitagraph trademark. *In Bridal Attire* (November, 1914) illustrated the troubles that might befall a prospective bridegroom who depends upon trolley cars and a motorcycle to take him to his wedding. *Billy, the Bear Tamer* (July, 1915) began with Quirk and Connie's father at odds. Dad banished the unwanted suitor and took his wife and Connie to Camp Stanley on a hunting trip so that he could keep an eye on his flirtatious daughter. Conspiring with Billy, Connie took along her pet pigeon, using it to fly a letter back to her beloved. Upon learning where she was, Billy formulated a clever plan and outfitted himself with the necessary items to carry it through.

Arriving near the cabin, Billy unpacked his bundle and produced a bear suit which he quickly donned. Crawling around a corner of the cabin, he revealed himself to Connie, who barely saved him from being shot by her father's guide. The guide agreed to become part of the plan and managed to extract the lead from the bullets in his client's rifle. While this was going on, Billy was busy tacking up signs, some giving notice of a penalty for shooting bears under fourteen feet in length, and others carrying the warning, "Beware the man-eating bear." The guide, leading Father out into the woods, persuaded him to overlook the signs until Billy appeared in his bear suit. Dad ran but recovered long enough to make a comic try at shooting the wild beast with the ineffective bullets. A chase back to the cabin ensued, and Connie was carried away by the bear.

In the woods Connie helped Billy out of the suit and he rushed back to the cabin, where his presence was less than welcome. However, when he offered to rescue Connie—provided the parents consent to their marriage—the distraught couple quickly accepted. Rushing back to the woods, Billy told Connie the news, ripped up his clothing, and the two staggered out of the wilderness, clutching the fake bear skin. As mother embraced Connie, father welcomed Billy into the family.

Directed by Lee Beggs for the most part, Quirk's comedies were amusing to view, but there was nothing outstanding about them or about his style of acting. His humor, like that in most of Vitagraph's comedies, often depended upon situation, and nearly anyone could have gotten the same laughs from his material. These one-reelers were used mainly as program fillers, for almost every important comedian was making double reels by this time. Billy had risen to prominence early but his career was fading even before the formative days of the motion picture ended. Other actors more aware of the vicissitudes of the public's taste surpassed him. Then, too, he was nearly forty and showed it; the type of roles he portrayed called for a younger man. Without a distinctive comic routine of his own, Quirk simply became one of the early casualties of the silent screen.

With Lubin, Selig, and Essanay, Vitagraph formed VLSE to release their features, but their short products still were issued under the General Film banner. The arrangement did not work, as Selig and Lubin resented Vitagraph and Essanay's calling the tune. Vitagraph bought out Lubin in September, 1916, and absorbed VLSE, allowing Selig and Essanay to withdraw.

Calling itself "The House of Comedy Hits," Essanay, almost from its beginning in 1907, set the pace for popular comedies. Ben Turpin had been hired that year, but his two-year stay with the firm was uneventful. However, the Essanay product came to be known for its snappy, crisp action and good technical work. Essanay never developed a major comedian of its own, but continued to grind out a steady diet of comedies, most of which were digestible and some even delightful, until its demise. The company's most notable success came with Chaplin in 1915. Chaplin by this time was already firmly established with the fans from the success of his comedies with Keystone (see Chapter 5).

In September, 1910, Essanay released a 233-foot comedy entitled *Joyriding*. This was the first effort of two comedians who came to be known to their screen fans as Hank and Lank. It proved to be so successful that several films were made for weekly release by the team. The films were all short and filled with good clean fun. Victor Potel and Augustus Carney played the roles, and once their box office appeal was established, they created new characters to fit into the Snakeville comedy series, which began in 1911.

Snakeville was a mythical village which provided the setting for many of the Essanay comedies. In this capacity, it performed much the same function as Lone Point in the later Kalem railroad series, *The Hazards of Helen* (1914). Off and on through the years, Snakeville remained the locale in many of Essanay's films, and, toward the end of the company's existence, it was regularly and prominently featured in its comedies. These were made by the Essanay western stock company under the guidance of G. M. Anderson, and even his famous character, "Broncho Billy," appeared in them.

Having proved his appeal in the Hank and Lank series, Augustus Carney created "Alkali Ike," a regular Snakeville character, and started his series with *Alkali Ike's Automobile* (May, 1911). He was supported in this one-reeler by William Todd as "Mustang Pete." In the film both loved luscious Betty Brown, the town's fairest maiden. Mustang invited her to go horseback riding and she accepted. Disgusted at being outwitted by his rival,

Ike caught up with them in his auto, and Betty deserted Pete for a ride in the flivver, which promptly broke down. Attempting to fix it, Ike inadvertently started the car, which roared off with Betty, leaving him to chase it on foot. The reel ended with the car dumping poor Betty onto the ground and Ike in grand disgrace.

This film was so popular that the next Snakeville comedy starred Todd, again as "Mustang Pete," in *Mustang Pete's Love Affair* (June, 1911). As usual, he lost out to Alkali Ike in the end. The two stars alternated as weekly attractions throughout the year. Perhaps the best explanation of their popularity lies in the simple appeal of the comic action. In *A Western Kimono* (February, 1912), Alkali Ike read of a new disease, Kimonitis, which the local newspaper warned was overtaking the female residents of the town. Ike, mistaking it for a genuine deadly disease, ran home to make certain that his wife had not caught it. Reaching home, he found a note to the effect that she had gone to town to have her kimono cut out. The humor in this one-reel film lay in the original error Ike made and in his frantic, slapstick efforts to reach town via a missed train and a railroad handcar, only to learn the truth.

Francis X. Bushman was making a name for himself in the field of light comedy as well as drama. At this time he was known as Frank Bushman, but as his ascent to stardom began, he reverted to the more dignified and formal Francis X. He lent his considerable talents and profile in support of the "Billy" comedies which starred John Steppling. In addition to these, he costarred with various Essanay actresses in comedies of his own.

The rather clever, but improbable, plot of *A Good Catch* (May, 1912) was typical. Bushman and Beverly Bayne portrayed an engaged couple having difficulties over money. He earned a living wage, but Beverly liked the good things in life, and an argument over a taxi ride broke up the otherwise happy couple. When a kind benefactor died, Frank started on his way to see the lawyer to claim the inheritance, but was arrested as a thief. It took a bit of comic doing, but he was finally released only to discover that the legacy was nothing more than an old photograph. When he showed it to his sweetheart, she recognized it at once as a picture of her dear Uncle John. In a flash, Frank got a bright idea and rushed her off to the lawyer's. Sure enough, Beverly was the lost heir and a large inheritance was waiting for her. The reel ended with the lovers taking the disputed taxi ride after all.

The emphasis which Essanay placed on comedy is seen in the April, 1912, release schedule. Of seventeen reels produced that month by the company, eight were slapstick comedies, half of all the comedies released that same month by the combined licensed companies. This kind of foresight paid off handsomely for Essanay. In the fall of 1912, Augustus Carney visited the Chicago studio for the first time in three years and was mobbed everywhere he went. Of course, the fact that he was wearing his Alkali Ike costume helped. He made several personal appearances, and a film of his visit was expanded into a comedy and released to the trade. A good part of Essanay's success in the comedy field was due to E. Mason Hopper, who directed many of the better films, including the "Alkali Ike" and "Sweedie" series. Hopper was a skillful and highly competent director whose ability to turn out films quickly earned him the nickname, "Lightning" Hopper.

Carney made a screen appearance in the role of Alkali Ike about six times a year, and by May, 1913, stores were selling Alkali Ike dolls for $1.50 each. These eleven-and-one-half-inch replicas of the character were mounted on a small hobby horse. Painstaking care had been given to detail. Essanay claimed that it paid $500 to have the face reproduced as lifelike as possible. After making *Alkali Ike's Gal* (August, 1913), a double-reel comedy, Carney went abroad, where he met with the same enthusiastic reception in Paris that he had received the year before in Chicago. While he was away, Essanay reissued his first Ike comedy of 1911, *Alkali Ike's Automobile,* and it was just as big a hit the second time around. Upon his return to the United States, Carney left Essanay for Universal, which had made him a better offer.

The Snakeville crew carried on, however, with emphasis on the character of "Sophie Clutts," created by ample Margaret Joslin. Her husband, William Todd, continued his portrayals of Mustang Pete in the series. These two were supported by Fred Church in the dual role of Coyote Simpson and Rawhide Bill, Victor Potel as Slippery Slim, and David Kirkland as Doc Killem. Together, they continued to turn out fine rural humor in a rather broad vein, but the Snakeville films, directed mostly by Roy Clements, were clean and entertaining, if not intellectually challenging. Today we would call them "corny."

By 1915 the quality of the Snakeville comedies had deteriorated as the quantity increased. Essanay's slogan by this time was "The first to standardize photoplays," and with the exception of the Chaplin comedies, their releases showed it. Another series which was released weekly in 1914 featured the character "Sweedie." Wallace Beery filled the leading role and spent most of his time in women's clothes. Feminine impersonation was popular with comics. Chaplin, Lee Moran, John Bunny, and Roscoe Arbuckle were all adept at portraying the weaker sex.

Beery had broken into the business supporting "Smiling Billy" Mason in 1913, and his Sweedie impersonations were in the same vein as *Countess Sweedie* (November, 1914). A real countess lost one of her calling cards while slumming in a hash house where Sweedie worked. Finding the card, Sweedie decided to "crash a party" that night and literally proceeded to do just that by falling downstairs in the middle of her introduction. The real countess arrived, the impersonation was discovered, and the police ousted the protesting Sweedie. Beery, although successful in this role, made a more charming villain for Sennett later on.

The last and best of the Essanay comedies were those in which Charles Chaplin appeared. Chaplin's request for a higher salary than the $400 Keystone had offered him was rejected by Sennett, so the young Englishman signed with Essanay in January, 1915, for $1,250 a week. The little comedian went to work for the Indian-head trademark and made fourteen films for Anderson and Spoor, all of which indicated his creative genius more clearly than his Keystones had. Also, he was now on his own, a different story from that of his career with Sennett. Whereas his earlier pictures had been filmed in a few days at best, Chaplin now spent as long as three weeks on a two-reel comedy.

Costing twelve to fifteen hundred dollars apiece, the Essanay Chaplins showed better construction in plot and continuity. His acting style and pace were slower and more refined. These comedies were a transition from the rough slapstick of the Keystones to the subtle pantomime of the Mutuals. They marked the introduction of pathos, irony, satire, and fantasy into his work. It was here that his tramp character came into full flower.

During his one-year stay with Essanay, Chaplin began to put together the group of supporting actors and technicians which he was to use so often in later years. Edna Purviance was discovered and became his leading lady for nine years. Leo White, Billy Armstrong, John Rand, James T. Kelley, and Charles Insley were prominent members of his company. But Chaplin's relationship with the management of Essanay was not harmonious, and he quit to go to work for Mutual in 1916. After he left for Mutual, Essanay padded his two-reel *Carmen* (April, 1916) into four reels by using discarded footage and cutting in a subplot with Ben Turpin. The company removed one entire sequence from *Police* (March, 1917) to pad *Triple Trouble* (August, 1918)—a film constructed by using scenes from *Police*, *Work* (June, 1915), and an unfinished feature entitled *Life*. To these were added scenes put together by Leo White in 1918, using doubles. Chaplin sued Essanay for tampering with *Carmen* and was countersued for alleged contract violation. The courts decided in favor of the company and allowed Essanay to release the film.[5] With the exception of a few Harry Watson, Jr. comedies made after joining Edison, Selig, and Kleine in 1916, Essanay released no other short comedies of note, preferring instead to concentrate on its feature programs.

Sigmund Lubin, the Philadelphia producer, had also gained early renown for sparkling, sharp, and interesting comedies. However, unlike Essanay, already well known for its comedies, Lubin's company was unable to sustain its reputation. Business was good for little "Pop" Lubin, who opened a brand new studio in April, 1910. He spent his profits to double the studio's capacity the following year, giving the company an investment estimated at above $500,000 for his plant and equipment.

Two Lubin releases of 1912 caught the audience's eye with their novelty. *The Lady Police* (January) featured a suffragette leader who was appointed chief of police by the mayor, who hoped for the female vote. The entire police force was altered with the addition of several comely lasses as officers of the law.

[5] For the best and most accurate description of Chaplin's work, see Theodore Huff, *Charlie Chaplin.*

Redoing the jail house to suit a woman's fancy, they refurnished the cells in the manner of rooms in a girls' boarding school of the day and soon had a waiting list of males eager to be arrested. When the cells became filled, the police station was picketed by angry wives who proceeded to take their erring husbands home, much to the dismay of the new police force.

A Midwinter Night's Dream (February) was cleverly put together. Lubin had a company working in Palm Beach, Florida, and parts were shot there to be added to the footage made in Philadelphia. The story concerned a tramp, asleep on a railroad freight car, who awoke to find the siding covered with snow. The mischievous little fellow threw a snowball which hit another tramp asleep in an orange grove. The scene shifted back and forth as the two tramps encountered two girls who agreed to meet them later downtown. On their way to the rendezvous the two tramps crossed paths with an actor who gave each a new suit. Inside a coat pocket, one tramp discovered a roll of stage money, and the girls and the tramps had a very merry time until their money was discovered to be phony. The inevitable chase dissolved into the ending as the tramp awoke to find a railroad detective waiting for him.

Lubin increased his output to five reels weekly in December, 1912. One release each week was a comedy, and *Peter's Pledge* (January, 1913) began a short-lived series starring Peter Lang. This was followed by a comedy unit under the direction of Arthur Hotaling. May Hotely starred and was supported by Raymond McKee and a host of other actors in a group of comedies known as "The Gay Time" series. These films depicted the good times one could have in various scenic spots and were more like travelogues than comedies, which is possibly the reason that they were not at all successful.

Throughout 1913–14, Lubin released split-reel comedies

made by the Hotaling unit, which remained intact longer than most comedy units. May Hotely stayed with the group, although the turnover in leading men was frequent. The unit traveled up and down the East Coast, from Philadelphia to Palm Beach, shooting pictures as it went along. A high percentage of these short offerings dealt with tramps, hoboes, and Negroes. As early as 1910, the company had released a short comedy with a character billed as "Rastus," and similiar films were released during 1914–15 with Luke Scott in the title role.

As Lubin neared the end of its existence, comedy efforts were more pronounced. Marie Dressler, fresh from her success in *Tillie's Punctured Romance* (November, 1914), was hired to star in five-reel comedies. Lubin finally announced two new policies in 1915. It decided to discontinue the split-reel comedies to concentrate on single reels with occasional features. Arthur V. Johnson, Lottie Briscoe, Ethel Clayton, and Joe Kaufman were active in some humorous releases, although they were essentially dramatic players. In April, Lubin at last recognized the aimless nature of much of its previous slapstick and announced to the trade that its single-reel burlesques and farces would have a purpose behind them. Coincident with this was the hiring of Billy Reeves and Jack Tucker to work in the southern studio under Arthur Hotaling's unit. Reeves had been a member of the Fred Karno touring company which had introduced Chaplin to the American public, and he had originated the part which his successor made famous. But his endeavors in the world of motion pictures failed to bring him the same fame.

The Selig Polyscope Company never paid a great deal of attention to comedies. After solving its early laboratory problems, the producer turned out mainly westerns and dramas, releasing four reels weekly. Each week, one reel was split with a three- to four-hundred-foot comedy. Selig's one brief attempt at continuity in comedy during 1912 was the adaptation of the *Katzenjammer Kids* (May, 1912) for the screen, utilizing live actors for the roles. Guy Mohler and Emil Nuchberg played Hans and Fritz, with Chauncey B. Herbert as the Captain, Lillian Leighton as Mrs. Katzenjammer, and John Lancaster as Uncle Heine. Technically speaking, the films were of high quality, but the effort lasted only a short eight weeks.

In 1913, Lillian Leighton supported John Lancaster in a series released as sporadic intervals featuring a genial, Irish hod carrier, Sweeney, whose dreams of grandeur were portrayed on the screen. That same year, a contract was arranged with Sidney Smith, the popular *Chicago Tribune* cartoonist, for the screen rights to his character, Old Doc Yak. Scheduled to be released as "Seligettes," the first of the intended series made its debut in July. It utilized a combination of live actors and animated cartoons but did not win acceptance at all. The animation work was poor and unsatisfactory, even for the standards of the time. The second six-hundred-foot reel was not ready for release until the end of October. This one was better received than the initial film had been. Selig kept improving its methods and releasing Yak comedies into late 1914.

It is doubtful that the cartoons ever earned enough to cover the immence amount of time and effort that went into creating them, but surprisingly, after six months' absence from the screen, Old Doc Yak reappeared. This time, the animation was as good as techniques would allow, for Selig had contracted with the Industrial Moving Picture Company to handle the mechanical effects as well as the photography, and the results were much more satisfactory.

Although the Selig company did little else with comedy, preferring to expend its efforts on westerns, especially the Tom Mix films (which had their share of comic elements), occasionally a

35

clever film was released that deserved more attention than it received. Such was the case with *Tobias Wins Out* (September, 1913). This humorous short reel established the character of Tobias as a soldier who schemed to get a discharge from the army by fair means or foul, only to be thwarted by a clever doctor until the very end.

Like Lubin, Selig appears to have directed much of its feeble comic efforts towards tramps, hoboes, and Negroes, but in 1915 the firm made two moves designed to strengthen its comedy program and to put it in a more competitive position. Selig established the Red Seal brand and in June hired Otis Harlan to star in the fall releases. It also announced a new series, *The Chronicles of Bloom Center*, to revolve around a typical rural village. This series featured Irene Wallace, Ralph McCormas, and Harold Howard and was intended to compete with Essanay's Snakeville comedies.

Release of the *Bloom Center* comedies was held up until a backlog of films could be produced, but troubles beset the unit from the beginning. The most pressing problem was finding a director who would stay with the stories. By the time the first film was released in October, four different directors had taken a hand in making the series: Burton King, Sidney Smith, Edward Le Saint, and Marshall Neilan.

One of Kalem's most notable failures was in screen comedy. Although founded in 1907, the company did very little with comedy until 1912, when split-reel western comedies starring Ruth Roland were released. Her first, *Hypnotic Nell* (May, 1912), told the simple story of a cowgirl who sent for a book on the fine art of hypnotism to win her man. This was followed by *Ranch Girls on a Rampage* (May, 1912) and a number of other films sufficiently entertaining to result in Miss Roland's receiving a better salary than she had previously enjoyed. Kalem's fear that Miss Roland's friendship with Mabel Normand might cause her to leave for Keystone may also have played a part in the salary increase.

The only other effort worthy of attention which Kalem made in screen humor came with the acquisition of Lloyd V. Hamilton, the principal comic of the Frontier brand. He was used in the Ruth Roland films, which for a time also starred Marshall Neilan. Bud Duncan joined the team, and Neilan took over as director. He used Hamilton, Duncan, and sometimes both with Miss Roland, as in *Ham, the Piano Mover* (November, 1914). In this film Bud did all the work for Ruth while Ham (Hamilton) offered advice and moral support.

Physically, Hamilton and Duncan were a Mutt and Jeff combination. They were both outfitted in grotesquely misfitting clothes, and poor Bud was always looking up to and admiring the wisdom of his six-foot partner. The usual reward for his adoration was physical disaster in the form of somersaults, dives through windows, numerous tumbles down flights of stairs, and a king-sized portion of kicks from Ham's elongated shoes. He took it all in stride with a zany nonchalance. Directed by Neilan, Chance E. Ward, and Rube Miller, the "Ham and Bud" series began officially with *Ham at the Garbage Gentleman's Ball* (March, 1915). When Miss Roland left Kalem, Ethel Teare took her place.

Kalem went into comedy production in a big way in its last three years in business. Frank Marion refused to invest a great deal of money in any film and successfully resisted the five-reel feature trend, if going out of business can be called success. However, the company did make a few three-reel films and even made a five-reeler, the successful *From the Manger to the Cross*. Ham and Bud continued their antics throughout 1915. While Lloyd Hamilton was out of action for a few months because of an injury suffered in rolling down a hill, Duncan and Miss Teare carried on alone.

Hamilton summed up the crazy world of slapstick comedy in 1915 with a reminiscence of some of his experiences: "In one film, I was attached to one end of a fifteen-foot rope which was, in turn, attached to a motorboat. Settling back, I expected a gentle jerk, followed by a pleasant ride into the cooling water and a pleasing imitation of a surf-boat ride. What I actually received was a violent yank, a cannon-ball flight through the air, ending as the whole Pacific Ocean rose up to meet me. I sank immediately and after an eternity, or so it seemed, I surfaced to hear my old partner, Bud, holler, 'Haul him out, we've reached China!' "

In January, 1916, Ethel Teare was starred in her own one-reel comedy series with Porter Strong, and Norma Nicholls replaced her in the Ham and Bud lineup. Harry Edwards came over from L-KO to direct the team from April, 1916, to March, 1917. In March, 1917, Ham and Bud signed another long-term contract with the General Film Company, and Al Santell was appointed their director.

In the meantime, Kalem had decided to replace *The Ventures of Marguerite* (1915) with a comedy series to be produced at its Jacksonville, Florida, studio, and after much effort finally signed Rose Melville. Miss Melville had portrayed Sis Hopkins (a sort of early Judy Canova) in the homespun rural comedy play of the same name. Frank Minzey, also from the stage version, was signed with her, and Robert Ellis was switched from dramatic to comedy direction. The first release scheduled was *A Flock of Skeletons*, in which Sis became a maid who was privy to all the family secrets, but the negative of this film met with an accident in the lab and *Leap Year Wooing* (March, 1916) became the initial release.

Edison was another of the pioneer firms that expended little effort in the comedy line. By 1912 its top comic was Gertrude McCoy, who did many fine things throughout her career but, like most of the Edison stars, suffered from her connection with the company. Edison regarded its players as little more than members of a stock company and, in this sense, expected each to be able to do a variety of things. This was fine, but as the star system developed, audiences came to expect certain players to portray certain types of roles. This assurance was noticeably lacking in the Edison release schedule.

A typical release which starred Miss McCoy was the single-reel *Every Rose Has Its Stem* (May, 1912). A young clerk (Barry O'Moore), who had fallen in love with a flower-shop girl (Bessie Learn), became fickle and turned his attentions to a cute stenographer (Miss McCoy), who had dollar signs for eyes. After losing all he had, the clerk gladly returned to the waiting arms of his first love. Like many of the other Edison comedies, this film came close to comedy-drama.

Herbert Prior, Mabel Trunnelle, Alice Washburn, Ed O'Connor, Dan Mason, Arthur Houseman, and William Wadsworth carried the company banner through 1913. The last two were to become the only real comics working for Edison. The company went overboard with its series idea, which had started with *What Happened To Mary?* in 1912. The bulk of its 1914 comedies, including *The Adventures of Andy*, with Andy Clark, a juvenile actor, and *Mr. Wood B. Wedd*, with William Wadsworth, retained this series format. Starting in December, 1914, Wadsworth and Houseman were teamed as Waddy and Arty in a weekly series of one-reelers.

One of the best films ever made by these two was *On the Lazy Line* (February, 1914), directed by C. Jay Williams. It began with a strictly melodramatic device—Grandmother's mortgage was due before 6:00 P.M. of a certain day. Her son (Herbert Prior) and his wife took the train on that day to reach the nasty villain's home. Unfortunately for them, they had to change trains and take the Lazy Line, which had only two cars —engine and caboose. Starting late as usual, engineer Waddy and Arty stopped a few miles down the track to refuel. Waddy handed Arty chips of wood so slowly that the hero became exasperated and did the job himself. They started off again, and even though the train was moving along at top speed, Arty was still able to carry on a conversation with Alice Washburn, who happened to be walking beside the track. With an indignant "I can walk faster!" grandson and wife stepped off the Lazy Line and, sure enough, they made it on time by foot, beating the train to the depot.

Edison did very little comedy in 1915 and, when VLSE was formed, combined with Kleine to take advantage of his distribution system. When VLSE broke up in September, 1916, Selig and Essanay joined the group and concentrated on feature pictures for the few remaining months before all left the business.

David Horsley, who had sold out his interest in Nestor to Universal, came back into the comedy field in 1915 as head of MinA Films. The films were produced in the Centaur studios for release by the General Film Company and Murdock McQuarrie headed the program. Harry La Pearl, a well-known circus clown, was also hired and proved popular with audiences. George Ovey came on in June until Horsley discontinued production in August. A disagreement between General Film and Horsley led the latter to form Cub with Milton H. Fahrney as director and to disavow all claims that he was associated with the films which General Film was still releasing as MinA. At the same time, Horsley resurrected Centaur and moved his releasing program to Mutual.

Vim comedies came on the market in November, 1915, as a replacement for MinA, courtesy of the General Film Company. Méliès' Manufacturing Company filmed the antics of Bobbie Burns and Walter Stull, who had formed Vim with Louis Burstein (or Burston, as he was later known). Burns and Stull portrayed Pokes and Jabbs and were supported by Ethel Burton, "Spook" Hanson and "Babe" Hardy. They added spice to the floundering program of General Film, and in April, 1916, Harry Myers and Rosemary Theby were brought into a second unit, with Kate Price and Raymond McKee joining in October.

The Pokes and Jabbs comedies contained the usual hobo slapstick whereas the Myers-Theby domestic comedies were better received by the public. Myers and Theby played a husband-wife team in well-produced films which, although they offered little in the way of marked story originality, pleased audiences. They opened their series with *Housekeeping* (July, 1916) and did one film a week until April of the following year, when both departed for Pathé following a shake-up in production. The Jaxon Film Company withdrew all Vim releases from the General Film program at that time, charging that it was losing money, and put them on the independent market, where they flourished until Jaxon and General Film shortly came to terms. Poke and Jabbs went back to General Film until 1918, when Burns dropped out of the series. Billy Ruge took his place, and the characterizations became known as Finn and Haddie. When Stull left, Oliver Hardy replaced him, and the series became Plump and Runt.

During 1916–17, General Film was so desperate for product that its policy requiring the total production output of a company was relaxed. Although the United States Supreme Court had handed down a decision favorable to Universal in its suit against the Patents Company (April, 1917), General Film had continued as a distribution outlet. The company announced readiness to accept any reasonable product for distribution, for by this time it received very few Selig and Kalem comedies, and only the Harry Watson, Jr. films from Kleine and Essanay. In 1917, General Film's major competition was as follows: Mutual had Cub, Vogue, and Strand; Universal released Nestor, Victor, L-KO, and Joker; Metro had the Drews, while Vitagraph had Larry Semon, Hughie Mack, and the team of Earl Montgomery and Joe Rock; Victor Moore was at Paramount; Essanay had Max Linder for a few films,[6] and Pathé handled the Rolin product. The leading independents were King Bee and Al Christie.

By 1918, Mutual had closed up Vogue, and Universal had discontinued Victor and Joker. Mack had left Vitagraph, and Linder was no longer active. With the breakup of Ham and Bud at Kalem, Duncan joined Dot Farley and Kewpie Morgan in a short-lived group of Clover comedies made by the National Film Corporation for General Film distribution.

[6] Linder's films for Essanay were failures but his earlier comedies made in France for Pathé had received much acclaim and established him as the leading French film comedian.

CHAPTER THREE

Universal's Challenge

NESTOR was formed late in 1909 by David Horsley. He was the same man who had previously founded the Centaur studio, which was dropped after a short, checkered existence but reactivated later. Horsley, who had come to the United States from England with his mother and his brother William, went into pictures by way of the back door. He had lost his right arm in a boyhood accident and this handicap made it difficult for him to find a job. Therefore, he opened a pool parlor and was successful in this enterprise until the Panic of 1907. His best customers were the ones hardest

43

hit by the economic recession, and business dropped off quickly. Like many other persons in similar circumstances, David Horsley was drawn to the motion picture field to get a fresh start.

In the meantime, his brother William had educated himself at night school and had become the superintendent of the Bigelow Company in Stamford, Connecticut. David lacked business sense, so he accepted William's offer of money and advice to help him survive in the rough and tumble world of movies. Together, the Horsley brothers forged an empire outside the Motion Picture Patents Company. The trust had refused Horsley a license to operate, but he was too far in debt to quit and the prospects of profit were too good to ignore.

Nestor's output as an independent producer was handled by A. G. Whyte of New York City. Whyte did so well from his New York office that he opened a Chicago branch in the spring of 1910. His profits from handling Horsley's product were good enough that Whyte, in partnership with George Graff, was able to form the Electragraff Company to produce Dandy Films. His second release, *An Interrupted Courtship* (June, 1910), was billed as an "excrutiatingly funny comedy. No repetitions or long drawn, agonizing chases over hill and dale." Dandy Films had excellent technical quality, but the plots and acting were below par and the brand soon became defunct.

Whyte next formed the Associated Independent Film Manufacturers, a company which released the wares of several other independents.[1] This exchange system soon collapsed. In the meantime, Nestor had continued to find favor with exhibitors, and Horsley built a new studio and laboratory in Bayonne, New Jersey, in 1910 to make possible an increase in production from one to two single-reels weekly. Like so many other enterprising

[1] Nestor, Centaur, Capitol, Motograph, Electragraff, Carson, Great Northern, Cines, Columbia, Eclair, Lux, Kinograph, and Thanhouser.

producers, Horsley moved quickly from comedy to drama and western films. Happily, there was one young man learning the art of comedy direction, and the name Al Christie was to have special significance in the future.

Nestor's greatest comedy successes at this time were in the exclusive contracts signed with Bud Fisher and Harry Hershfield. Fisher sold the rights to his comic strip creations, Mutt and Jeff, and served as adviser while others wrote the actual stories. The pictures began as one-reelers and were billed as "talking" pictures. More aptly, they should have been called "titletalking" pictures, for superimposed on the bottom of each frame was a caption appropriate to the scene. William Horsley had devised this touch to add punch to the humor. Real actors took the roles, but their names were never revealed to the public.

Beginning with *Mutt and Jeff on the Job* (July, 1911), thirteen full-reel films were made, followed by twelve split-reel comedies. They were released weekly until November, 1911, when the *Desperate Desmond* series was created from the cartoon characters of Hershfield. Real actors were also used in the six split-reel offerings about this Victorian-age villain before both series were discontinued in favor of strictly dramatic fare. In later years, Horsley claimed that Mutt and Jeff had cleared $60,000 during their short existence. It is interesting to note that Nestor would turn from westerns back to comedies before 1912 ended.

In October, 1911, production had been expanded, this time to a schedule of three releases weekly. Tom Ricketts, later to become an important figure in the firm, was added to the staff of directors. A former scene-shifter on the New York stage and a cousin of David Horsley's wife, Al Christie was straining at the leash to produce more comedies. He was put in charge of the "Wild West Weekly" series in mid-1912 at a salary of $35.00

a week. The series was based on stories found in a pulp magazine of the same name and was frowned upon by the exhibitors, who complained that patrons read the magazine and stayed away from the theaters. In August, Christie's unit changed over to western comedies, and Louise Glaum was put to work along with Donald McDonald and Ed Lyons. When Miss Glaum left ten months later, Evelyn Quick was hired from the Keystone ranks to replace her.

From the time that the Associated Independent Film Manufacturers Company failed, Nestor had been part and parcel of Carl Laemmle's Motion Picture Distributing and Sales Company. When the Mutual Film Corporation was formed in 1912, Horsley had an opportunity to sell out, but he decided to stay in business and to keep his affiliation with Laemmle. The relationship between these two men was an intricate blend of friendship and finances.

The Motion Picture Distributing and Sales Company had been formed in 1910 to market the wares of independents and to marshal assets for the fight against the trust. Each member turned over its release prints of new subjects, which were then marketed by the Sales Company for $100 a reel. Of this sum, $95.00 was returned to the producer of the member company, which then paid a stipulated fee for the selling service performed by the Sales Company. The remaining $5.00 was retained by the Sales Company as an assessment toward fighting the patent war which David Horsley had initiated in the courts. This assessment was charged on every print handled, whether for thirty different subjects or for thirty prints of the same film. The immense sum of money needed for the patent fight may be realized when it is considered that $650 was withheld weekly from the sale of the Nestor product alone.

John Bunny worked at Vitagraph and became one of the first
famous film comedians.

In this building at 900 Broadway, Bayonne, New Jersey, twenty-two feet wide, fifty-two feet long, on a lot one hundred feet long by twenty-five feet wide, David Horsley started making motion pictures in 1907 under the name of Centaur Film Company.

Courtesy Mary Horsley

Neal Burns has a feeling that marriage is too close for comfort
in *Oh Promise Me,* an Educational comedy.

Courtesy Sam Grossman

Certain scenes were often duplicated in the silent comedies. The one above is from an early Sennett short. Compare it with the picture at the right.

Courtesy Nick Fiorentino

This scene with Eddie Condon from *Captain Suds*, a 1925 Century comedy, utilized the same background as the picture on the left, but with a variation in theme. In the decade between the two photos, a railroad track and more utility poles appeared.

Courtesy Don Overton

Waddy and Arty, the leading Edison comics, in a scene from one of their cinematic escapades.

Courtesy Howard Nelson

Fay Tincher, the leading
female star of the Mutual
Komic program, in the
striped dress that she
made famous.

Courtesy Howard Nelson

Edgar Kennedy has Roscoe "Fatty" Arbuckle cornered as Louise Fazenda looks on in *Fatty's Tin Type Tangle*, a 1915 Keystone comedy.

Courtesy Howard Nelson

Harry Aitken shared the power with Laemmle, but this state of affairs shortly became a free-for-all over which one would retain control. Harry Aitken had arrived in New York in the spring of 1911 to take over the ailing Hudson Film Company. Changing its name to the Western Film Exchange of New York, he went into distribution. Under his guidance, the doors of the Majestic Film Company opened in November, 1911. Tom Cochrane, who had organized Imp for Laemmle two years before, was retained as general manager. This move was made possible by the absence of Carl Laemmle, who had gone vacationing in Europe with the thought that all was well at Imp. Aitken took advantage of his absence to raid Laemmle's company and to acquire much of its talent. His coup was topped by the acquisition of Mary Pickford, the most prized actress at Imp, at a salary of $275 a week. She brought along her husband, Owen Moore, and they starred in the firm's first release, *The Courting of Mary* (November, 1911).

Roy Aitken (brother to Harry) was the manager of the Western Import Company of London, which handled the foreign sales of both Majestic and Reliance. The latter had been formed by Charles Bauman and Adam Kessel and had started production in October, 1910. Bauman raided the Biograph studio and acquired the services of Arthur V. Johnson, Marion Leonard, Henry Walthall, Gertrude Robinson, and James Kirkwood. Reliance films were strictly dramatic[2] and so were the Majestic releases until Roy Aitken replaced Cochrane in the spring of 1912. T. Hayes Hunter was brought in at that time as director, and Mabel Trunnelle and Herbert Prior, two popular Edison

---

[2] They were until 1914, when a single reel weekly was added to its output. This was the *Two Men and a Mule* series about the escapades of two tramps and one mule. The mule did not appear after the first release.

comic personalities, were lured into the fold. They were to rejoin Edison at the end of the year, but contributed some fine
moments of hilarity under the Majestic banner.

Aitken contended that there was a shortage of comedies on
the screen, and how true this was! He proposed, by way of
remedying the situation, to release split-reel comedies along
with the regular dramatic fare. However, his plans regarding
comedy were not realized, and Edward Apfel of Edison was
hired in August to direct and strengthen the release schedule.
Apfel established a stock company—much as Edison had—and
Laura Lyman headlined the comedies during 1913.

Also during this time, the relationship between the Aitkens
and Carl Laemmle had become one of increasing animosity. As
Laemmle was the dominating figure in the Sales Company, he
was in a position to retaliate against Majestic for the raid which
had cost him the services of Mary Pickford. This he accomplished by requiring Majestic to pay a higher percentage to
the Sales Company than the other members. Aitken filed a com-
plaint against the Sales Company as a combination "in restraint
of trade" and, with ten other firms from the Sales Company,
split to form the Film Supply Company of America.[3] The split
left Laemmle with seven companies under his wing. With his
own company, Imp, Laemmle combined with Edwin Porter and
William Swanson's Rex brand, P. A. Powers' firm of the same
name, and Kessel and Bauman's New York Motion Picture Company to form Universal.[4]

Shortly afterward, another disagreement arose between Kessel and Bauman, on the one hand, and Laemmle, on the other.
It resulted in Bauman's withdrawal from Universal, leaving

[3] The company distributed for Thanhouser, Lux, Gaumont, American, Great
Northern, Eclair, Reliance, Solax, Majestic, and Comet.

[4] The other three firms were Champion, Republic, and Nestor.

the brand name of 101 Bison and $17,000 in Laemmle's hands. The Kessel and Bauman product—Keystone, Broncho, and Kaybee—went to the Mutual Film Corporation, which had been formed in March, 1912, by Aitken and John R. Freuler. The Film Supply Company had simply been a stop-gap measure while Aitken made overtures to Crawford Livingston and Kuhn, Loeb and Company, Wall Street investment bankers. Once financial support was assured, most members of the Film Supply Company joined Mutual. This new alliance of independents announced a policy of purchasing products for distribution from the Mutual exchanges, regardless of the affiliations of the producers.

By 1913 the only remaining American firm releasing through the Film Supply Company was Solax. The history of this firm is unique, for it was the first American motion picture company formed, owned, and operated by a woman. Alice Guy and her husband, Herbert Blaché, a pioneer motion picture director, had arrived in the United States in 1907 to help launch the Gaumont Chronophone, an early form of talking picture which had been developed by the prominent French manufacturer of photographic equipment. When the Chronophone process did not catch on with the public, Gaumont decided to establish an American studio in Flushing, New York. The Blachés were placed in charge of this operation. Madame Blaché had been involved with motion picture production in France with Gaumont. She opened the Solax Film Corporation at Fort Lee, New Jersey, in the fall of 1910 and directed many of its releases, proving to be a capable director in her own right.

The best of the Solax comedies were made with Billy Quirk, a thirty-five-year-old Jersey City comedian. Quirk had previously worked for Biograph, where he had supported Mary Pickford, played straight dramatic roles, and made a series of comedies portraying a character known to the public as "Muggsy." In this respect, he was already established with the public and had a solid reputation. At Solax, he often played with Darwin Karr, who was to become a minor legend for his fine dramatic portrayals. Lee Beggs, who was later to direct Quirk at Vitagraph, also supported him in his Solax comedies, with Fannie Simpson and Blanche Cornwall providing the feminine interest.

Quirk's first Solax release, *Hubby Does the Washing* (February, 1912), pitted Quirk against Blanche Cornwall as the wife who constantly complained about washday. Billy, not one given to false economy, took up her dare to take in washing, and the rest of the single reel showed his trials and tribulations with the home laundry equipment of the day. While his comedies were both popular and profitable, Quirk often stepped out of character to do drama, as in *Fra Diavolo* (July, 1912) and *The Blood Stain* (August, 1912), for which he received notable reviews.

He left Solax in late 1912 for Imp, but was not put to work until early 1913, when he was shifted over to Gem, another Universal brand. There he was supported by Billie Baier, but the stories he was given to work with were weak and Quirk was not inventive enough as a comedian to overcome them. *Billy's Troubles* (March, 1913), was his first single-reel Gem.

The Film Supply Company still had its foreign product,[5] but the company was in trouble. Many new companies were entering the production field, and distribution of their products was hastily taken over by the failing organization.[6] The attempt to salvage the firm was of no avail, however, and the enterprise went under. Out of its wreckage came the Exclusive Film Corporation, which for a time handled the release of Great Northern, Blaché, and Solax, plus miscellaneous features.

[5] Gaumont, Ambrosio, Great Northern, Itala, Lux.
[6] Ammex, Ramo, All Star, Monitor, Magnet, Anchor, Prairie, and Comet.

Laemmle had his own troubles. Shortly after Imp was founded in 1909, he had sent Ben Turpin to California to seek a suitable location for filming away from the surveillance of the trust. Turpin had returned to report that California did not seem to be the place, for Biograph and Selig were already making pictures there. The signing of Mary Pickford as an Imp star at $175 a week had so angered Biograph and the Patents Company that Laemmle decided a trip to Cuba was in order. This removed Imp from the jurisdiction of the United States courts, a move deemed necessary until the situation became calmer. Laemmle's production in California did not begin until after the formation of Universal, when he took over the Hollywood studios belonging to Nestor.

About the only comedies of note that Imp ever produced were made in 1912–13. Four units went into action in July, 1912, to shoot split-reel comedies. Two of the units were under the direction of Fred Mace, the Biograph comedian who had decided to stay behind when Griffith headed back east with his troupe in June. The other two units were under Edward Le Saint and featured Harry Pollard, Margarita Fischer, and Virginia Kirtley. During 1913, King Baggot, the reigning Imp favorite, alternated between comedy and dramatic releases.

The films of genuine comedy value which Universal released did not come from Imp but rather from three other sources. P. A. Powers' firm released a number of wholesome comedies, such as *The Great Towel Robbery* (August, 1913) and *The Pearl of the Golden West* (September, 1913). One of Powers' best comedy releases while this firm remained active centered around a fine series of burlesque which Allen Curtis made during 1915. With all the solemnity of a high-powered serial, *Lady Baffles and Detective Duck* poked fun at the more serious screen fare. Gale

Henry and Max Asher co-starred in these eleven one-reelers, which first reached the screen in January.

The meat of Universal's comedy films at this time was supplied by the Crystal Film Company, formed in 1912 by Joseph A. Golden. Pearl White was hired from Pathé in September, 1912. She had been with Powers in 1910, and her popularity at that time had caused the company to issue a calendar with her portrait on it. At Pathé, she had almost dropped out of sight. With Chester Barnett as her male lead, Miss White began work at Crystal, her first release being *The Girl in the Next Room* (October, 1912), a comedy of mistaken identities and lost letters. Eight months later, her sterling reputation led Crystal to feature her in two single reels weekly, starting with *Where Charity Begins* (May, 1913).

Although a comedy favorite, Miss White longed to make dramatic pictures. Discontent and overwork caused her to leave Crystal in 1913 for a vacation abroad. She had no idea that a few months after her return, she would find everlasting fame as the first and greatest of the serial queens. After eight weeks abroad, Pearl returned to Crystal to continue making her popular comedies. The trip abroad had refreshed her and had restored her outlook on life. One must work at what is interesting to be happy, and Pearl was interested in movies, whether serious or comic. She continued with Crystal until signing the contract with Eclectric which led to *The Perils of Pauline* (1914).

Crystal comedies continued to be popular, and in March, 1914, the firm expanded to two full reels weekly. Vivian Prescott, who had played in Imp and Biograph comedies, was hired, along with Charles De Forrest of the Imp "Binks" series, to make the second reel each week. Nestor, too, continued to put out good comedies. In 1914, Al Christie, coming closer to the day when he would head out on his own, was making two-reelers with Ed Lyons, Lee Moran, John Steppling, and Ramona Langley.

By December, 1913, Universal was releasing thirty reels weekly of its different brands, ten of which were comedies. Laemmle had founded Joker to produce comedies exclusively, and its first release was *The Cheese Special* in October, 1913. The Joker brand, which replaced the old split Imp, was conceived to counter the growing influence of the Keystone comedies. Max Asher, an Oakland, California, boy whose specialty was German characterizations, played the leads. Louise Fazenda and Harry McCoy supported him, with Allen Curtis directing.

The Joker comedies featured a low form of humor, even including the actors' spitting on each other from time to time, among other inelegant actions. *Traffic in Soles* (February, 1914), a burlesque of the then popular white slave films, was particularly offensive in its treatment of decaying fish in a fish market. Bobby Vernon was added to the cast in mid-1914, and Asher left to join Sterling in October.

Regardless of their style of humor, Joker comedies were popular, and a second unit was formed in February, 1915, under the direction of Archer McMackin, who stayed only one month before joining American. Ernest Shields, Eddie Boland, and Bertha Burnham were with the unit from the outset, with Milburne Moranti soon to appear. Universal continued to release the Joker brand until 1918. Two fairly representative examples of Joker humor during this period were *Hubby's Cure* (January, 1915) and *One Damp Day* (June, 1917). In the former, Louise Fazenda attempted to cure her husband (William Franey) of his drinking habit by rearranging the furniture prior to his coming home drunk. In the latter, Franey wanted a divorce from Gale Henry and filed the necessary papers. In a mix-up in a restaurant he got the wrong coat, and as he left, he found a paper in the pocket which caused him to believe that Gale had inherited a large sum of money. His haste to retract the divorce papers provided the basis for the comedy which followed.

The speed with which Universal expanded its comedy program during 1914 was bound to affect its product—and it did. The company was rapidly becoming nothing more than a factory grinding out what it called comedies. Each succeeding release looked as if less attention had been paid to it than the last. *How Green Saved His Mother-in-law,* a Joker release of April, 1914, was typical. Its big scene cut back and forth from the street to a window in a burning building. In some shots out of the window, the woman wore a kimono, in others she wore a dress. Strange as it may seem, such inane errors were often overlooked by audiences.

The acquisition of Augustus Carney from Essanay in January, 1914, marked the beginning of a long series of raids by Laemmle on other lots employing comedians. Harry Edwards was assigned as director, and the Universal Ike brand came into weekly existence with the release of *Universal Ike Gets a Goat* (March, 1914). Louise Glaum was hired to support Carney, but by May a misunderstanding had arisen between Edwards and Carney. Ike packed up and moved off the Universal lot, but his leaving did not disturb Laemmle, who put another actor in the role, billing him as Universal Ike, Jr. In this manner, he continued to cash in on Carney's popularity with unsuspecting audiences until viewers realized that they were being duped.

Henry ("Pathé") Lehrman and Ford Sterling left Keystone to join Universal in the second of Laemmle's raids. Robert Thornby, a Keystone director, "Little Billy" Jacobs, a juvenile star, and Fred Balshofer of the New York Motion Picture Company completed Universal's haul. Balshofer was put in charge

54

of the Sterling brand. Its first release was a two-reeler, *Love and Vengeance* (April, 1914).

Sterling was a La Cross, Wisconsin, boy who ran away from home at the age of seventeen (in 1897) to join the old Robinson circus. Billed as "Keno, the Boy Clown," he banged around the boards for some time before joining Biograph in 1912, where he met Sennett. In his early Sterling releases, he created the character of "Snookee," which was similar to his portrayals at Keystone. Emma Clifton supported him in a way which led viewers to mistake her for Mabel Normand. Imitation is the sincerest form of flattery, as Chaplin was to find out, but it was also annoying at times.

Soon after he began production, Ford took a vacation and returned with Teddy Sampson, an occasional player for various Mutual affiliates, as his wife and new co-star. The Sterling release schedule was one reel a week, and the monthly program consisted of two Ford Sterling and two "Little Billy" Jacobs comedies. The Sterling brand lasted only slightly more than one year. When Sterling left to rejoin Keystone in January, 1915, the unit continued producing with Johnny Brennon, Lloyd Ingram, and William Wolbert, but it had been kept solvent by the films which Ford made. Billy Jacobs moved over to Majestic, and the Sterling Company closed its doors in May, 1915.

Henry Lehrman, not one to share the limelight if it was unnecessary, left the Sterling Company in October, 1914, to form his own brand, Lehrman–Knock Out, or L-KO. He established four producing units and hired former circus clown Rube Miller, George Nichols, and Harry Edwards to direct with him. L-KO released through Universal. Its best-known comic was a small and ineffective Chaplin imitator, Billie Ritchie, who soon ran afoul of his more gifted model. Louise Orth provided the feminine support, and Hank Mann joined the group in May, 1915.

L-KO comedies were out-and-out imitations of the Keystones in both style and stories.

The L-KO brand lasted long after Lehrman departed, taking Ritchie with him. The Stern Brothers, Laemmle's nephews, acquired the firm, and quality, which had not been too good anyway, declined still more. It soon became fashionable in the industry to comment derisively on the L-KO comedies, and Julius Stern was touchy about the jokes concerning his films. One well-remembered occasion found Stern the brunt of more remarks than he could bear, he lashed out angrily at his critics with the now-famous remark, "L-KO comedies are not to be laughed at!"

Alice Howell was the best known of the L-KO comic stars throughout its existence. She left in the spring of 1917 to make Century comedies on her own for independent release. J. G. Blystone, the general manager of L-KO, produced these for Miss Howell on the side and began the series with *Balloonatics* in June, 1917. Buster Keaton was later to use the same title and a similar plot in one of his famous shorts.

The Stern Brothers became associated with the Century banner, and release then went to Universal. Miss Howell left the company, and the Century comedies became a showcase for animal antics. L-KO was discontinued in July, 1919, to be replaced by the Sterns' Rainbow comedies. At this time, Universal had only two other comic releases—Nestor with Sammy Burns as lead and the comedies of Lyons and Moran.

Eddie Lyons and Lee Moran had appeared in many Nestor films together, but they were not really a team until 1915. Al Christie was doing strictly comedy work by this time, but one Nestor unit was under the direction of Lyons until the front office decided to team him with Moran. Horace Davey took over as director, and Lyons and Moran quickly became one of the top money-makers for Universal during 1915–17.

In *When the Mummy Cried for Help* (January, 1915), Moran agreed to pose as a mummy to oblige his friend Lyons, who was trying to pass himself off as an expert on Egypt. Ed's problems with his girl friend, Victoria Forde, were nothing compared to the hilarious headaches Moran gave him. In order to win her hand, Eddie had to revive a mummy which her father had acquired from a curio shop. The father had discovered what he believed to be the elixir of life. To solve the problem, Eddie called in his chum to take part in a grand deception, which worked beautifully. Unfortunately, a group of Egyptians found out about the experiments and, thinking Moran to be the real mummy, stole him. The chase was on, but soon ended satisfactorily for everyone. The professor was certain that his elixir worked, the Egyptians got back their mummy, and Eddie won Victoria.

Eddie's Little Love Affair had Lyons cast as a professor in a school attended by his sweetheart (Elsie Gleason). Moran, a fellow student, was continually trying to get Eddie in trouble with the dean by accusing him of flirting with his students.

Betty Compson was discovered by Al Christie in 1915. She had been playing a vaudeville sketch in Los Angeles while touring the Pantages circuit. Christie cast her at once in *Wanted, a Leading Woman*. Her role was that of a movie queen whose affections were sought by both Lyons and Moran. As the reel ended, both boys learned that she preferred Gus Edwards, a midget. Miss Compson had a stellar career ahead of her in the twenties.

Management difficulties were brewing at Universal, and Al Christie wanted out. In January, 1916, he began to produce his own films for Universal on a footage basis, using the Nestor name. Leasing the studio, he made forty reels before quitting to form the Christie Film Company, which William Horsley helped finance. Christie's last picture for Universal was *Wanted—A Husband* (June, 1916). When Christie left Nestor, he took Betty Compson, Stella Adams, Neal Burns, and Lyons and Moran. The last two, however, were offered the opportunity to make their own films for Universal, and they returned to the Nestor banner.

An amusing and typical Nestor comedy of June, 1917, is a prime example of the Lyons-Moran style of humor. *War Bridegrooms* had the boys celebrating on the eve of Eddie's wedding. In the process of making merry, they were arrested and sentenced to the rock pile. To cover up this disgrace, they sent word home that they had been drafted. Returning in purchased uniforms, both were acclaimed as heroes until the local sheriff discovered that they still had two days left to serve, when back to prison they went. Rosemary Theby joined Nestor in August, 1917, to play opposite the team.

Their films continued to be popular with the audiences. They had developed a style of comedy somewhere between slapstick and polite humor, managing to combine the burlesque of one with the realism of the other. They kept in motion constantly, for movement was a dominating factor in their production ideas. Both men felt that the audiences paid to watch them move, and they kept the tempo at a steady pace. Their views paid off, for they were one of the oldest and most popular teams in motion picture comedy, first under the direction of Christie and later on their own.

Christie's first production for the independent market, *A Seminary Scandal* (September, 1916), starred Billie Rhodes in the story of a girl who went off to boarding school. Her beau couldn't bear to part from her, so he went along too, disguised as a girl, and the stage was set for fun. Christie's formula for comedy was similar to Lyons' and Moran's. Their ideas had more or less evolved together during their long association, and

58

Christie was to make these ideas profitable for a long time, even into the era of sound.

With the notable exception of the Christie unit before it began independent production, no comedy and no comedians of importance were developed by Universal. Carl Laemmle's objections to the contrary, the company could hardly be considered a major source for comedy during its first ten years of existence. Although comparable to much of its competition of the time, the Universal product had an assembly-line monotony that was not to disappear until the mid-twenties. There was little that was unique or outstanding about the bulk of the firm's releases. Much of the blame must rest with Laemmle, whose philosophy of production and tight rein on the budget helped stifle creativity.

CHAPTER FOUR

"Mutual Movies Make Time Fly"

THE split in the Motion Picture Distributing and Sales Company, which had resulted in the formation of Mutual, for a time gave this organization the release rights for the most popular comedies in the nation, the Keystones. These, along with the series of Lone Star comedies made by Chaplin, were the best of the limited Mutual comedy program. Having acquired the Keystone, Broncho, and Kay-Bee product almost at the outset of its existence, Mutual, in a manner typical of the early film industry, went after its next acquisition. A balanced program had to be made available to exhibitors if the firm was to grow and prosper. This responsibility went to Charles J. Hite, a second vice-president and director of Mutual. Representing a syndicate containing his partners J. R. Freuler and Harry Aitken in the American Film Manufacturing Company, Hite set his sights on a firm which could provide the dramatic fare needed by Mutual. His target: the Thanhouser Company.

Edwin Thanhouser's auspicious beginning had been marked by the release of *The Actor's Children* (March, 1910), a one-reel comedy-drama. Refused a license by the trust, the former actor decided to go independent and hired Lloyd Lonergan to do the scenarios. Frank Crane, Anna Rosemond, Orrilla Smith, and Yale Boss made up his opening roster of performers. Yale Boss was to join Edison the next year, where he successfully played juvenile roles for a number of years. Thanhouser quickly dropped comedy, save for an occasional release in which comedy was incorporated rather than dominant. The company soon became well known in the industry for its technical excellence.

As business increased rapidly, Thanhouser had to devote more time to company operation and less time to the creative end of production. Demand for his films became so great that by early 1912, he had three units hard at work—one each in Florida, Niagara Falls, and New Rochelle, New York. Finding that Thanhouser was willing to come to terms when properly approached, Hite bought the plant and all assets of the Thanhouser Company for an undisclosed sum. The syndicate promptly reincorporated as the Thanhouser Film Corporation and installed its founder at the helm as general manager. Thanhouser remained in this capacity for only a short time before he retired from the business and left for Europe.[1]

[1] After a lengthy stay abroad, Thanhouser returned to the United States with the intention of establishing a film laboratory service. When Charles J.

61

Another firm which fell under the Mutual banner for release of its productions—again, largely because of Hite's efforts—was the American Film Manufacturing Company. As president and general manager of the Theater Film Service Company, Samuel S. Hutchison had been connected with the motion picture industry almost from its beginning. When the Motion Picture Patents Company was formed, Hutchison had declined to participate. Pressure was applied by the General Film Company, and he was forced to sell out. He then went into partnership with Charles J. Hite, and the two men began to do business with the independent producers as the H. & H. Film Service Exchange. In October, 1910, they formed American with A. M. Kennedy as general manager.

Three shooting units were provided, and the new company occupied the studio of the defunct Phoenix Company while its facilities were being constructed. Dot Farley was engaged as the star of the comedy unit, and the first release was *Romantic Redskins* (November, 1910), a western comedy. Humor was part and parcel of American's release schedule until April of the following year, when production was restricted to the J. Warren Kerrigan unit, which produced two westerns weekly for more than a year.

Split-reel comedies came back into American's program with *Hidden Treasure* on November 30, 1912. Early in that month, the eastern producing unit had been disbanded and was replaced by a new studio at Santa Barbara, California. Wallace Reid, later a star in his own right, was brought in to direct the additional productions. Young Reid was only twenty-three at

---

Hite was killed in an automobile accident on August 22, 1914, Thanhouser was prevailed upon by Mutual to head again the firm bearing his name. Thanhouser accepted and on September 1, 1914, assumed the responsibilities held by Hite.

Soon to become a star, Gloria Swanson played opposite her husband Wallace Beery (from whom she was separated at the time) in *Teddy at the Throttle*, a 1917 Sennett comedy.

Courtesy Nick Fiorentino

Ben Turpin's big break came as a foil for Chaplin in Charlie's
first two comedies for Essanay. The above impassé occurred in
His New Job (1915).

Courtesy Nick Fiorentino

As usual, Ben Turpin is in a bad way in this scene from *A Night Out* (1915), an early Chaplin Essanay. Charlie is on the left, sympathizing with his companion.

Courtesy Howard Nelson

Charlie Chaplin has just lost a scoop of ice cream and is quite put out by the mishap in *The Adventurer*, the last of the Lone Star Mutual comedies.

Billy West, the most successful of the Chaplin imitators, is about to make short work of Leo White as Rosemary Theby nervously watches. This scene is from *Bright and Early,* a 1918 King Bee comedy directed by Charles Parrott, later to become famous as Charlie Chase.

Dot Farley, the "ugliest comedienne on the screen," had two pro-
truding front teeth that dominated her features when she smiled.

Lupino Lane, the fabulous acrobat, in a posed studio shot at the peak of his screen fame with Educational, near the close of the silent era.

Author Lahue interviews E. Mason Hopper, a director in the
silent era and a veteran of more than forty-five years in pictures.

the time, but he had worked for Vitagraph, Reliance, and Imp in the two years that he had been in the picture business.

The most successful of the American comedies was the "Calamity Anne" series, created by Allan Dwan for the new unit. Louise Lester was hired to play the leading role, with Lillian Christy providing ingénue support. This off-and-on series of western comedy-dramas found favor with the exhibitors, not only because of the technical excellence of the American product, but also because of the quality of the stories and the acting. Miss Lester's reputation acquired luster by the occasional appearance of popular Jack Kerrigan as co-star in many of her films.

At the beginning of 1914, the Beauty brand was instituted by American, with Margarita Fischer, Harry Pollard, and Fred Gamble doing light social comedy-dramas. Much care was taken in the production of these films, and they lived up to the trade name in both technical quality and scenic views. Pollard and Fischer stayed busy well into 1915, but gradually the comic interest declined in favor of drama as films became longer. Other Mutual interests had been created to take over the production of comedy.

When D. W. Griffith took his Biograph winter company back east in June, 1912, Fred Mace stayed behind. He did some work for Imp before joining the original Keystone Company. Very popular at Keystone, he quit Sennett in March, 1913, to organize his own firm with release through Majestic and Mutual. He started out to produce a comedy series about the mishaps of a punchy boxer, "One-Round" O'Brien, a character he had created earlier in a Biograph release. A genuine pugilist, "Bull" Young, was hired to lend color and flavor to the portrayals. Young played a fighter whom O'Brien bribed to throw the match. O'Brien then started dating his opponent's girl, only to find that Young did not consider her part of the bargain. This was made clear to our hero as his bribe backfired and he was flattened in the first round.

The "O'Brien" series had limitless possibilities, but unfortunately, Young also fought in real life, and shortly after production began, he was knocked cold by Jesse Willard and died as a result of the injuries he suffered. Mace could not replace him and closed shop, moving over to Apollo, where he acquired Bud Duncan as a foil. He made a few films and many plans, eventually leaving Apollo to start another company of his own. Leasing space in the Majestic studios, he opened the Fred Mace Feature Film Company, but returned to Sennett in July, 1915. In one of those strange switches common to the early days of movie-making, Edward Dillon leased space in the Reliance studio and released his comedies through Apollo, thus filling the void left by Mace's departure.

In 1915, a schism appeared in the Mutual Film Corporation, and Harry Aitken withdrew, taking with him the Reliance-Majestic product (meaning Griffith), and combined with Thomas Ince and Mack Sennett to form Triangle. Thus Mutual was left without a notable comedy unit, and the grouping of its dissident elements under the Triangle banner put Mutual at a distinct disadvantage. Samuel S. Hutchison established the Signal Film Corporation in October for the sole purpose of exploiting the serial aptitude of Helen Holmes and J. P. McGowan, whom he had lured away from Universal. At the same time, he formed Vogue with Charles La France to produce comedies for the ailing Mutual program.

La France gathered together a unit composed of heavy (300 pounds) Russ Powell, Lillian Leighton, Priscilla Dean (as ingénue), Milburne Moranti, and William Scott (light comedy). In the meantime, M. E. Spero had formed a company to produce

Kuku comedies with Dot Farley and Sammy Burns under the direction of Gilbert P. Hamilton.[2] Kuku comedies were for the independent market and began with *Sammy's Scandalous Schemes* (December, 1915). Although the two-reelers were free from vulgarity, the first two releases had Burns the exact double of Harold Lloyd's "Lonesome Luke" (sans moustache) and doing a poor imitation of Chaplin.

La France and Hutchison had a disagreement and dissolved partnership. This left Hutchison with Vogue and nothing else. Until he could acquire a new unit, he contracted to release the Spero films under the Vogue name. This placed *Sammy vs. Cupid*, the third Kuku, in the Mutual schedule. Paddy McGuire from Essanay was one of the first of the new Vogue players. Hutchison also gained the services of Jack Dillon as director, along with Rube Miller, formerly with L-KO. Lillian Hamilton and Gypsy Abbott completed the list of principal funmakers. Ben Turpin and Edward Sedgwick joined the company in April, 1916, and the Kuku comedies returned to the independent market.

The one-reelers—the only films made at first—were received well enough that in June, Vogue began turning out double reels. Two months later, the company split the single unit which it had been using for production and made it into two. Rube Miller became director of Unit Number One, for Dillon had departed. Roy McRay was assistant director, and Ben Turpin, Miss Hamilton, and Harry Huckins headed the cast. The second unit was directed by Henry Kerman, with Jack Gaines as his assistant. McGuire, Art Moon, Ed Laurie, and Gypsy Abbott handled the acting. Margaret Templeton was added to the cast for variety near the end of 1916.

Lillian Hamilton achieved moderate success as the feminine

---

[2] Sammy Burns was another English comic who had done acrobatic and gymnastic comedy on the British stage.

interest in Turpin's comedies. Only eighteen years old, this petite lady had done juvenile roles at Morosco's Burbank Theatre before entering pictures with Selig in 1914. Adept at both comedy and drama, Miss Hamilton had worked at Universal and Premier and with Al Christie prior to her debut at Vogue.

J. R. Crone, the manager of Vogue from its inception, left in December, 1916, and was replaced by James Davis, former director of *The Hazards of Helen* (1914–1915) for Kalem. The following month, Rube Miller's contract expired, and he left the firm. The two units were recombined, and Robin Williamson came on as director. George Ovey, a comedian under the Cub banner, was scheduled to make a few Vogue comedies, but the burden fell upon Turpin and McGuire, who appeared together and separately in some double-reel comedies. Davis was unable to please Hutchison and, within a month after he replaced Crone, was sent into the field as a director. A. E. Stone of the Flying A brand was brought over to handle the affairs of Vogue until its demise in the late spring of 1917.

Of the Komic brand films made for Mutual release, the most interesting ones featured Fay Tincher, who had appeared in the "Billy" series for Majestic in 1914. Miss Tincher played Ethel, a gum-chewing stenographer, with Tod Browning in support. Edward Dillon directed these comedies, and Ethel, in her black-and-white-striped dress, became a welcome sight on the theater screens of the nation.

Edith Thornton and other members of the Crystal stock company came under the Novelty brand, a new company formed by Mutual. Novelty films arrived on the market for the first time on October 4, 1915, but they did not last long. Horsley's Cub comedies featured diminutive George Ovey as a slapstick comedian called Jerry. His one-reelers met with great success, and he was kept busy doing regular weekly releases for more than

66

29359

two years, until he left Horsley for the independent Gayety in 1919.

Other than the Keystones, the two most popular Mutual comedy series were the Strand shorts and the comedies of Charles Chaplin. Chaplin had joined Mutual in February, 1916, after much fanfare, and the Lone Star Film Company was established to film and release his series of twelve two-reel films. Chaplin was at the height of his creative ability during 1916–17, when he made a dozen near-perfect shorts in only eighteen months. Although there were to be many later pictures in which Chaplin's genius would be evident, never again in his career would he make so many brilliant films in so brief a period. After leaving Mutual, his comedies became longer and required much more time to create.

Chaplin had refined his early techniques so that his acting showed a new maturity. His films at Mutual were to be the foundation for the remainder of his career, for time and again he borrowed ideas from them to use and expand in his later features. His salary and bonus, totaling $670,000 for a year's work, along with the production costs, brought each of the Mutuals to about $100,000 in total cost. This figure, which exceeded the cost of other comedy products of the day by many, many times, even went above the cost for features.

Chaplin's Mutuals had clear plots and themes, along with the satire, pathos, and irony he had first introduced in his Essanay films, but they exhibited a more mature talent. The slapstick in them was a natural outgrowth of the situations, not something thrown in or added for good measure. It is impossible to pick out a "best" Chaplin Mutual, for all of them have something distinctive about them. Some critics have called *Easy Street* (January, 1917) his best, but surely *The Pawnshop* (October, 1916) equaled it in every way. *One A.M.* (August, 1916) was rare, in that Chaplin did a solo performance except for one brief scene at the beginning with a taxi driver. In *The Rink* (December, 1916), Chaplin demonstrated his unparalled grace and agility, for much of it took place on roller skates. He spared nothing in making his films as good as he knew how. Roughly 90,000 feet of film were edited into the 1,809-foot *The Immigrant* (June, 1917), and it took him eighteen months to complete his one-year contract.

Chaplin's Mutuals were tremendously popular, and the exhibitors paid up to fifty dollars a day for them when they were first released. As time went by, their rental rate rose surprisingly. Usually, the rate became lower as the film grew older. Five hundred prints of each were distributed, compared to the average fifty to one hundred of other comedy products. Essanay reissued its Chaplin films at the same time to cash in on the exhibitor and audience interest which the Mutuals had created.

The Strand comedies opened in April, 1917, with *Her Hero*. Billie Rhodes and Jay Belasco took the leads in these one-reel films produced for Mutual release by the Caulfield Photoplay Company. The ninth of the series, *A Two Cylinder Courtship* (June, 1917), was one of the best, combining elements of polite comedy with elements of slapstick. Unable to overcome Billie's father's objections to their marriage, Jay and Billie decided to elope. Prior to starting, Jay drained most of the gasoline out of the father's car, but father saw them and a wild automobile chase ensued. Just as the chase was getting exciting, dad's car stalled. Thwarted for the time being, he called lawyer Jones in the next town. The lawyer disguised himself as a minister and managed to trap the lovers in a hotel room. While he went for the father, Jay and Billie made a rope of blankets, which they lowered out of the window; then they hid. When dad arrived, he was puzzled by the rope and wondered if they had managed to escape. While he was trying to figure it out, Jay and Billie ran from their hiding place and locked him in the room. On the street below, they met a real minister, and father, watching from the window, became an unwilling witness to the ceremony.

Strand continued making comedies into 1919 with Elinor Field and Henry Depp as stars. Miss Field was a seventeen-year-old who had done one season of comedy stock after graduating from high school in Los Angeles. These films were made by the Southern California Producing Company, with Scott Sidney directing, and began with *What Will Father Say?* (August, 1918).

Many of them were clever in concept, such as *'Twas Henry's Fault* (June, 1919). This comedy reflected the ridicule and respect accorded Henry Ford's flivver and incorporated through subtitles several of the current jokes that were a part of every Ford owner's life. At breakfast, Harry and Betty discussed their preference in automobiles. Harry admired the Wildcat Roadster, while Betty favored the Duplex Sedan. Alas, the couple had no money for such a luxury, and Harry left for work at the office. After he had gone, Betty got a bright idea. Going to the piano, she removed her hoard saved from the grocery money and decided to buy what she could with it.

Dashing into the office later, Betty informed Harry that he now owned a car, and his fellow workers congratulated them both. Harry stepped out to inspect his new car, and his co-workers' praises quickly turned to derisive jokes. Disappointed, Harry didn't know what to do or say until the boss arrived and broke up the inspection party. Betty pleaded with him to let Harry go for a ride on office time, offering a home-cooked meal for them all that night in return. At this, the boss relented, and the couple started off, to the hoots of their friends.

The flivver quit on the road, and Harry, disgusted with the whole thing, took a bus back to work. Betty managed to start it again and set off for a ride in the country. As the gang came in for the free supper, poor Betty was back in the country sitting in the flivver, which had broken down once more. While the men were preparing their own supper, Betty was walking home. Harry's friends finally gave up after burning the meal and stalked out, leaving him to witness his wife's arrival with an old beau who had happened along and given her a lift. Harry refused to listen to her story and a quarrel followed, after which Betty sneaked out to hire a mechanic to fix the car.

Missing her later, Harry thought that she had gone to meet his old rival, and he started out on foot to square accounts. As the rival fled in his car, Harry jumped into his employer's parked car and a wild chase began, ending when the borrowed car broke down. Along came Betty in the repaired auto, and her point was made—any car can break down. Harry got in beside her, and they happily towed the other vehicle back to town.

Cheerful little comedies such as Strand produced made good program fillers but had little chance of prospering under the Mutual banner and expired when the highly touted Mutual flag fell. After Mutual lost Keystone, the Strand comedies and the films of Chaplain were the best of a much less successful lot handled by Mutual over the years.

CHAPTER FIVE

Keystone Kapers

MUCH has been written, both fact and fiction, about the formation of the Keystone Film Company by Kessel and Bauman of the New York Motion Picture Company.[1] Let it suffice here to say that Keystone was officially announced on August 12, 1912. The original company consisted of Mack Sennett, Ford Sterling, Fred Mace, and Mabel Normand. Mace was already in California when the others arrived

---

[1] For various discussions of this, see Gene Fowler, *Father Goose,* and Mack Sennett and Cameron Shipp, *King of Comedy.*

on August 28 to start work in the old 101 Bison studio in Eden-dale which had been turned over to Keystone.

Contrary to most published accounts, the first Keystone released to the theaters was a split reel on September 23. The titles were *Cohen Collects a Debt* and *The Water Nymph*. The supposed first Keystone release, *At Coney Island*, was actually a split-reel release of October 28.[2] The story has often been told that the group stepped from the train in California and encountered a parade. According in this legend, Sennett thrust a rag doll into Mabel Normand's arms and Mabel promptly rushed out into the parade, pleading with one of the marchers while the camera caught it all. In reality, this was the release for October 14, entitled *Stolen Glory*, and was made some four weeks after the troupe had arrived.

The Keystones were immediately successful with exhibitors, and Sennett found that business was good enough to warrant organizing a second unit in February, 1913. Henry Lehrman directed, and Betty Shade was the female lead. By June, Keystone was releasing full reels along with the split ones and, at the close of the year, had seven directors turning out three single reels weekly with one two-reeler each month. In less than a year, Sennett had become the talk of the industry, Mutual's most important product source, and a direct stimulus to Universal's vast comedy expansion.

What was there about the Keystones which made Sennett such an instant success with the public? His name became synonymous with slapstick and chases, even though both had their

---

[2] Ford Sterling played the lead in the Cohen series and his brand of wacky and exaggerated slapstick was very popular. Behind the full beard (which later diminished to the tuft beard that Sterling made famous) was a comedy actor with talent. He was able to put feeling into his comic portrayals, which brought forth both sympathy and affection from the audiences. He quickly became the top comic on the Keystone lot during 1912–13.

origins in France and were used here before he came on the scene. Sennett's contribution can best be explained by saying that he added an American flavor and refined these two types of comedy by slowing down the camera and adding absurd touches. Except for Mabel Normand and Chaplin, every member of his motley stable of comics was absurd in some respect: Roscoe "Fatty" Arbuckle, cross-eyed Ben Turpin, leering Mack Swain, impish Chester Conklin, pathetic Harry Langdon, and so on down the list. Even Chaplin's screen character, as it developed in his Keystone films, contained absurd elements which were later reduced to more human terms as he polished his portrayals.

Sennett realized that if one policeman was humorous, a group of them would be riotous. He gave the world its zaniest police force, and one you wouldn't dare call if you were in trouble— the Keystone Cops. Pretty girls were also essential in Sennett's brand of comedy. A dozen luscious girls fawning over Ben Turpin was a guarantee that the house would come down in an uproar. Custard pies flew all over the place, cops fell headlong into mud and water, cars careened crazily along the edge of cliffs and plowed through houses, motorcycles mowed down pedestrians, and buildings exploded with regularity as Sennett went about his business. Without a doubt, this man was responsible for creating more laughter through the years than any other individual in the world. Through the doors of his "Fun Factory" poured laugh after laugh.

The evolution of his best-known contribution to the art of screen comedy came about slowly. A short release of April 24, 1913, started it all. In *The Bangville Police,* a pretty girl believed burglars to be in her neighborhood and called the rural police. Their tribulations in answering this call for help soon became standard screen fare in many Keystones, with Fort Sterling as their chief. The process of development continued and was high-

73

lighted in January, 1914, with *In the Clutches of a Gang*, a two-reeler which to this day remains the funniest comedy ever to feature the Keystone Cops.

Many stories have circulated about Sennett's callous attitude toward his Cops, who went through everything imaginable for a laugh, but it must be remembered that nearly every Keystoner was experienced in the art of falling, slipping, sliding, and so on. They knew their business. Hence, the public marveled as the clowns tumbled on, providing thrill after thrill and laugh after laugh.

From the silent comedy short has come many classic situations: the beautiful girl bound to a table as the buzz saw bears down upon her, or the city slicker enticing the country girl to go to the big city with him. Actually, these situations were not used as commonly as the stereotype would lead one to believe, but used they were indeed, and in the best of the Keystones.

Mabel's Awful Mistake (May, 1913) was one example—the story of a villain who enticed the beautiful and trusting country girl with the promise of marriage. When she learned that he had a wife and children, she decided to return home, but the would-be bigamist and double-dyed villain had no intention of letting her go. No sir, he strapped her to a planing table in a sawmill and turned on the saw. Fortunately, her country-boy lover (Sennett) appeared on the scene as always, in the nick of time (amidst many chuckles)—to hold back the machinery bare-handed until help arrived.

Barney Oldfield's Race for a Life (June, 1913) was another classic, but had more drama than humor, although we probably wouldn't think so now. Complete with moustached villain (Ford Sterling) and country rube (Sennett), this film was made to take advantage of Oldfield's reputation as a race driver. Sterling wanted Mabel, but Mabel loved Mack. Since villains hate "No"

74

for an answer, it was no surprise when Mabel got chained to the railroad track as Sterling bore down upon her with a locomotive. Sennett and Oldfield gave chase in Barney's racer, passed the train, and Mack freed Mabel. The police arrived on a handcar and Sterling shot them all, but there was still Mack to contend with. Running short of bullets, Sterling choked himself as the reel ended.

Leading Lizzie Astray (November, 1914) gave Roscoe "Fatty" Arbuckle, who had been hired to replace Fred Mace, and his wife, Minta Durfee, another of the classic plots with which to work. When a city dandy's car had a flat, along came Fatty with Minta and volunteered to fix the tire. While he was doing that, the dude played up to Minta. The big city sounded good to Minta, who wasn't very happy with Fatty's hayseed kin, so off she went. Later, Fatty put his necessities in a handkerchief tied to a stick, said goodbye to Mom and Pop, and set off after her. Meanwhile, Minta had been getting rough treatment from the dandy, who was really a cheapskate, and his extravagant friend (Mack Swain). That evening at a cabaret, Minta was again getting the worst of it from the dude, when Fatty suddenly broke in and displayed his own strength by knocking a few heads together. United once more, Fatty and Minta returned home.

Arbuckle was a triple-threat man for the Keystone studio. Not only did he act, he also wrote and directed some of the more hilarious comedies released by Sennett. One such, *The Alarm* (May, 1914), should be seen to be fully appreciated. The entire two reels were devoted to the rivalry between a country police force and the fire department, which ended only when the fire engine plunged over a cliff, much to the delight and glee of the merry policemen.

The construction of any early Keystone comedy, 1912–15, was a joy to behold. The script was often written after filming was completed, simply to enable the cutter to edit the film properly. Beginning in 1915, this concept of production was abandoned in favor of an increasingly rigid method which required following a detailed script while filming. However, in the early days, all those connected with a certain comedy unit (and Sennett had twelve by 1916) would gather and have a sort of round-table discussion. An idea would be suggested; it was passed around among those present. Each would add or alter the idea until a suitable outline was agreed upon. Its evolution was a fascinating example of the best minds in the business at work. By the time they left the studio to begin shooting, the group had a pretty good idea of what the general plot would be.

The writing staff—and Sennett did have one regardless of stories to the contrary—would then whip up a scenario which was submitted to Sennett, who supervised the bulk of the pictures made at his studio.[3] His stamp of approval on the outline cleared the way for hilarity, but it did not necessarily mean that the script would be followed to the letter. Karl Coolidge, who was later to write some interesting serial scripts, resigned as story editor in May, 1913. He could not take life in the Keystone madhouse any longer.

For example, in *A Tugboat Romeo* (November, 1916), it was suggested that Chester Conklin portray the captain of a tug. Here was the germ of an idea. The logical question followed: "What can he do as a tug captain?" The idea, of course, was to get as many laughs as possible. Perhaps a fall would be suggested: "Man overboard, it's the captain!" How was he to fall overboard, and why? So it went, and the story was soon completed. Once the basic outline had been established, shooting,

---

[3] In the beginning Sennett directed the comedies himself, but by 1914 the company had grown too large for one man to handle all of the footage which went out under the Keystone banner.

76

could begin. Improvisation played an important part in the film-ing, for the best falls, stunts, and comedy sequences often origi-nated from a haphazard but inspired moment. No wonder vis-itors to the Sennett studio thought that everyone was mad!

The weather also played a large part in the shooting sched-ules of the early days. A single reel could be turned out of the Keystone madhouse in a week or less—a two-reeler might re-quire up to two weeks—but adverse weather could really throw the schedule to the wind. Shooting a picture outdoors could be done only in bright sunlight, because of the slow emulsion of the film. Artificial lighting was coming into use, but it was not yet satisfactory and created as many problems as it solved. It was not unusual for a comedy unit to sit around for weeks, shooting only a few feet of film a day because of poor light. L-KO was barely able to make its release schedule during the rainy season of 1915, for it had only an outdoor studio at the time. The tug-boat film took three months to make at Balboa. The fog was terrible from August through October. When the unit arrived there, the season was in full swing. When they finally left, every-thing was tightly boarded up. The cast went for as long as ten days at a time without turning the camera crank.

The schedule of releases had to be met. Sennett, along with all other producers, had definite commitments for his pictures, and if the schedule fell very far behind he was in trouble. Since weather was the critical factor, an attempt was made to work far enough ahead of schedule to have a backlog of films. When weather permitted Mack pressed everyone possible into service to build the reserve. After one lengthy winter of rain and bad weather, Sennett approached William Campbell, a writer, and said, "Bill, you're going to direct. We've got to get pictures out." Campbell replied, "Mack, I can't direct, I'm a writer." The final word on the subject came back like a rifle shot, "You're going to learn to direct, get busy!" Many men at Keystone got their start in this manner, and Sennett seldom missed his schedule.

Charlie Chaplin was hired in the spring of 1913 by Adam Kessel. Ford Sterling had been voicing discontent with his salary, and it was feared that he would quit at any time. Chaplin was receiving fifty dollars a week for his role with the Karno Company, then touring the United States. Kessel's offer of a contract which guaranteed him $150 a week for an entire year was too good to pass up, although Chaplin had a few qualms about making the move. His commitment to Karno did not allow him to join Keystone until December, 1913.

Arriving at the Keystone lot, Chaplin was assigned Henry Lehrman as director, and they set about making his first film. *Making a Living* (February, 1914) was far from the Chaplin we recall today. With monocle and droopy moustache, dressed in a long frockcoat and wearing a high silk hat, Chaplin tried to resist the frantic Keystone style of acting and clashed frequently with Lehrman, but to little avail. Soon only Mabel Normand felt that the little Englishman had any promise as a film comedian.

The beginning of his famous costume and the introduction of his shuffling walk came with the second film, a split-reel called *Kid Auto Races at Venice* (February, 1914), shot off the cuff in a very short time. But Chaplin's opportunity to prove to Sennett that no mistake had been made in hiring him came with his addition to the cast of *Mabel's Strange Predicament* (February, 1914). Clashing again with Lehrman, he was given his chance by Sennett, who turned the picture over to Chaplin. In this film Charlie introduced his now famous corner skid and soon had the set roaring with laughter. Turning a sharp corner, he skidded, holding one foot out straight and balanced on the other, at the same time looking back while clutching his hat.

Sennett began to realize that Chaplin would do better on his own, so, starting with his thirteenth film, *Caught in the Rain* (May, 1914), Charlie wrote and directed all of his own pictures. They became a combination of the Keystone style and his own ideas. When he entered pictures, Chaplin had had no idea how films were made, but he devoted much time and effort studying motion picture technique. His time proved to be well spent.

The Keystone Chaplins consisted of thirty-four shorts and one six-reel feature, *Tillie's Punctured Romance* (November, 1914). These films—except for the feature, which took fourteen weeks to make—were improvised for the most part on the spot and were filled with slapstick and some vulgarity. Chaplin's screen character in these comedies was still not the Charlie we remember so fondly. He was basically a sharper and often a thief and a drunk. The mature Chaplin did not appear until his year at Essanay. The mannerisms developed during this year—the shuffling walk, the swinging cane, the foot resting on someone else's lap—were to be refined as time went on.

Generally, a Chaplin comedy of the Keystone era left much to be desired when compared with his later work. It is the comic bits and pieces found in each that make them worthwhile viewing. In a few places, one notices a look or a gesture that anticipates Chaplin's introduction of the human element into his work, as in *Twenty Minutes of Love* (April, 1914), which had Charlie tenderly embracing a tree after watching a couple kissing on a park bench.

The best known of all Chaplin's Keystone comedies was the six-reel *Tillie's Punctured Romance*. Although Marie Dressler had been brought in from the legitimate stage to star in the film, it was Chaplin who caught the fancy of the public when it was released. Miss Dressler, in spite of several sequels made for other companies, failed to attain real success in pictures until the thirties, when she became one of the top attractions in the early sound era.

Chaplin's thirty-four short comedies have over the years been recut and reissued under no less than ninety-seven different titles. Unfortunately, each recut and reissue has brought further destruction of the talents he exhibited. The originals contained few and brief titles. The new editions were padded and "pepped up" by the addition of new, verbose, and often tasteless titles. Sometimes whole sections of films have been deleted or otherwise destroyed, so much so that an unmutilated original does not exist, to my knowledge, even in the hands of a collector. The same is true of many of Chaplin's other films.

Charlie's comedies brought a new dimension of popularity to the Keystone product. From all over the world, letters poured in asking for information and pictures. His popularity increased with each succeeding release. By 1915, when he moved to Essanay, Chaplin's future showed unlimited promise.

The year 1915 found Keystone more successful than ever. Sennett, with the exception of Chaplin, had rounded up the cream of screen comedians under his banner. His roster of stars that year read like a Who's Who in Screen comedy: Ford Sterling, Mabel Normand, Chester Conklin, George J. (Slim) Summerville, Fred Mace, Mack Swain, Eddie Foy, Polly Moran, Louise Fazenda, Charlie Chase, Raymond Hitchcock, Harry Brooks, Don Barclay, Harry Booker, Francis Wilson, and Billie Walsh, among others. Charlie Murray, a Biograph personality formerly under the direction of Del Henderson and at one time one-half of the vaudeville team of Murray and Mack, joined. So did Harry P. Gribbon, a comic star of the Gayety Musical Stock Company. Even the famed Weber and Fields signed a contract. They had previously been associated with the World Comedy Stars Film Corporation under a long-term agreement, but the firm did not last. This year the original Keystone company hit its peak and Hampton Del Ruth, as scenario editor, had more than enough to keep him busy. By September the firm had laughed itself into a brand new $100,000 studio.

Many of the best 1915 Keystones featured Roscoe "Fatty" Arbuckle. The rotund comedian was to continue to add to his reputation until the tragic scandal of 1921. At that point, his career ceased, but while he was active and loved by the audiences, Arbuckle played in a number of fine and funny films. *When Love Took Wings* (April, 1915) was a one-reeler which had all the speed and dash associated with Keystone. Poor Fatty was one of three love-sick young men who wished to elope with the same girl. The action was immediate as one tried to elope by motorcycle, only to lose his love to the second in an automobile, who in turn lost her to the fastest of the three, an aviator (Arbuckle). Like all the best Keystones, it *moved* from beginning to end.

Arbuckle and Normand often played together as husband and wife. In *Fatty and Mabel's Married Life* (February, 1915), Fatty, against Mabel's protests, stepped out for a while. The queer movements of a curtain soon had Mabel on the verge of collapse. Certain that the Black Hand was after her, she called the police—none other, of course, than the faithful, regular, old-fashioned Keystone police force. Against great odds (themselves) and in the wake of much merrymaking, they finally arrested the culprit—an organ grinder's monkey.

The best film by Arbuckle and Normand in 1915 was *That Little Band of Gold* (March, 1915). In a mere two reels, it portrayed the two as man and wife, then as divorcees, lovers, and again as man and wife. This rapidly paced film opened in an opera house with Fatty sharing a box with Mabel and his mother-in-law. The latter's critical presence made everyone uncomfortable, and Fatty became increasingly irked by her as the evening progressed. In the opposite box sat Ford Sterling with his girl— and a prudish chaperone. Disgusted with the entire affair, Fatty and Ford's girl sneaked out together. Later, Ford called Mabel, who started divorce proceedings. Fatty, however, became remorseful and began courting Mabel again. The two fell in love all over and were remarried in one of moviedom's wackiest ceremonies. A mere outline of the plot hardly does justice to this fine comedy, for many of the laughs came from the profuse, yet subtle expressions of the cast.

Not all of the Keystones were grand successes. *A Versatile Villain* (May, 1915) starred Charlie Chase and Louise Fazenda in the story of a dainty bandit who was finally cornered and blown up with a dynamite storehouse. Not only was the story bad, the action was ineffective and poorly timed, and it looked as if one of Sennett's directors had left suddenly while it was being made.

The Triangle Film Corporation, formed in July, 1915, by Harry Aitken, drew its name from the three producers involved —D. W. Griffith, Thomas Ince, and Mack Sennett. Its formation came about from the dissension in the Mutual Film Corporation. Freuler and Hutchison had been feuding with Aitken for some time over management of the firm. Freuler lined up support, and at the June election of officers, he was chosen to replace Aitken as president, a post he immediately fortified by buying 720,000 additional shares of outstanding Mutual stock. Aitken withdrew his Reliance and Majestic product and persuaded Kessel and Bauman, the backers of the Ince and Sennett films, to do likewise.

Triangle immediately announced a new and daring policy. Seats in the theaters showing its pictures were to go for two dollars each. The company imported a large number of stage stars and went to work, opening at the Knickerbocker Theater on September 23, 1915, with Sennett's *My Valet,* starring Raymond Hitchcock, and *A Game Old Knight,* with Charlie Murray, as the first contribution. Within three months, Triangle claimed that five hundred theaters in the United States had signed up for its program. Participating theaters ran the Triangle releases exclusively; many split the weekly program in half, using the Griffith-supervised feature and one Keystone for the first half of the week, then closing out with the Ince feature and the second Keystone. Throughout 1916, Sennett made two comedies a week, but announced a cutback to one each week in January, 1917, coupled with a statement that his Triangle films could now be booked by any theater, regardless of its affiliation with Triangle. This announcement alone was an indication that all was not well at Triangle, and trade suspicions were confirmed when Griffith left the fold three months later.

Sennett's Triangle comedies were not much different from his earlier Keystones. He utilized many actors from the stage, such as Joe Jackson, Eddie Foy, Sam Bernard, and Weber and Fields. Foy and Sennett did not get along and Eddie soon walked out, after appearing in only a few comedies. Because of his contract violation, Foy's later suit for his last week's salary was unsuccessful. His only Triangle, *A Favorite Fool* (November, 1915) was a two-reeler with Polly Moran, Mae Busch, and Charles Arling. Eddie appeared as a tramp who married a widow, only to learn that she had seven children (his own Seven Little Foys).

The Best of Enemies (December, 1915), also in two reels, marked the debut of Weber and Fields, soon to depart for greener pastures. This film cast the duo as German comedians who were attempting to break into society. When Weber disappeared mysteriously, Fields was accused of murdering his friend because of their social rivalry. Tried, convicted, taken to the death house and then to the scaffold, poor Fields had a one-two count from the hangman when Weber suddenly came around the corner and stopped to watch the proceedings. Recognizing his friend's jeopardy, he stopped the execution just in time and with a good deal of comic action. Chester Conklin and Mack Swain provided most of the genuine humor as supporting actors in the Weber and Fields comedies.

The stars came and left Sennett with monotonous regularity. Fay Tincher, best remembered as Ethel, the gum-chewing stenographer in the Komic comedies, joined in May, 1916. In December of the same year, Fred Mace departed for good, reportedly for the legitimate stage. Fatty Arbuckle landed a Paramount contract and left Sennett in January, 1917. Mabel Normand decided that she was ready for feature comedy work and prevailed upon Thomas Ince to star her in five-reelers.

Like the Keystones, Sennett's Triangle comedies were fast, furious, and frantic in both action and movement. Two of the best were *The Great Vacuum Robbery* (December, 1915), and *Bucking Society* (April, 1916), both double reels. In the former, Edgar Kennedy and Louise Fazenda decided to rob a bank by crawling down the hot-air channel and sucking the bank notes from the vault with a vacuum cleaner. Charlie Murray, a detective in female disguise, followed them to a summer hotel. "Slim" Summerville went along as his assistant. These two boys were such keen detectives that unless a suspect was over three years old, he couldn't fool them! Once they were all at the hotel, a long series of pursuits in and out of rooms, through skylights and over rooftops took place until the money finally wound up in the hands of its owner and the two crooks were apprehended.

William Campbell directed Chester Conklin in *Bucking Society*. On his way to Shorty Hamilton's wedding, Chester was hurled out of a freight car but snagged on to the hook of a mail crane, where he awaited the next train. Finally arriving at the scene of the ceremony, he discovered that Louella Maxim was out only for his friend's money and he wildly shot up the place, suspending the wedding for all time. The trick photography (not uncommon in Sennett's films) made the freight-car scene appear genuine, and Campbell's fine work proved that he *had* learned to direct.

One other comedy of note came out of the Triangle association. The U.S. Navy graciously provided a submarine at the San Diego Navy Yard, and Sennett sent a crew to make *A Submarine Pirate* (December, 1915). Sydney Chaplin, the half-brother of Charlie, was given the lead in this four-reel comedy, and he made the most of it. Sydney had been responsible for Charlie's job with Karno and had accompanied him to Hollywood, where he helped direct his brother's new career and also made a few films for Sennett. In this absurd comedy, Sydney was cast as a waiter who secretly wanted to be a juggler and practiced on the job. Overhearing Glen Cavender and Wesley Ruggles plotting to capture a bullion ship with the aid of a submarine, he bought a second-hand admiral's uniform and took command of the sub. It was laugh after laugh as Sydney went after the bullion ship himself. He finally succeeded in sinking it, but the sub was damaged in the process. The film ended with a bit of underwater mirth, as Sydney shot himself out of the torpedo tube of the dying submarine. The film received rave reviews at the time of release and was popular with many patrons. Sydney had a wacky although somewhat vulgar style of comedy, and this film remains his best screen effort of the period.

In July, 1917, Sennett departed from Triangle, leaving behind the Keystone name and trademark. At this time, enough Keystone-Triangle comedies had been made to carry the release through to October. Sennett signed a contract to release via Paramount, then went on vacation. Triangle promptly established two groups of comedies: one-reelers under the Keystone banner and two-reelers labeled Triangle Comedies. A few of the lesser lights had remained with Triangle, and production began of comedies bearing names which the public associated with Sennett. It is fair to say that these bogus Keystones did not begin to compare with the originals.

Sennett had retained his executive staff as well as most of his players, and he organized four units under Eddie Cline, Victor Herrman, Fred Fishback, and Clarence Badger. He did not assign his actors to a particular director as in the past, but put them on call for any director who wanted them. His release program called for one double-reel film every second week.

By this time, a change in the audience's taste for comedy had become apparent to him, and his films of this period, although no less risqué, were slower paced and more deliberate in character delineation.[4] A good example is found in his first Paramount release, *A Bedroom Blunder* (September, 1917), which starred Charlie Murray as a henpecked husband vacationing with his wife (Eva Thatcher) at a resort. Charlie was carefully built up as a fellow who had little chance to exercise his own mind and who did just as his wife expected. Of course, the beach was crowded with bathing beauties, and Charlie was interested mostly in the view, while his wife complained about their accommodations. When she discovered what was occupying his attention, she pulled the curtain down with a flourish and turned around, back to the window. The curtain pull caught on the bottom of her dress and, sure enough, went to the ceiling, pulling her dress over her head. From outside the window, the

---

[4] Although the name Sennett is synonomous with pie throwing, this had been abandoned in all but a very few instances by 1918. Sennett had grown beyond this elemental form of slapstick.

86

camera caught the last of the scene, showing a broad expanse of bloomers.

This film was followed by *A Pullman Bride* (October, 1917) with Gloria Swanson, Mack Swain, and Chester Conklin. The third release featured Polly Moran, "Slim" Summerville, and Ben Turpin in *Roping Her Romeo* (October, 1917). One of the best films that Sennett produced under the new contract was *Watch Your Neighbor* (March, 1918). It had Charlie Murray as an undertaker who split his daily receipts fifty-fifty with "Dr." Wayland Trask. Mary Thurman was the good doctor's wife. Charlie had a wandering eye, and the antics he employed to steal his partner's wife, while reassuring the poor fellow that he meant no harm, were hilarious. With this kind of situation as a basis for plots, almost anything could happen and often did.

In a few short years, Sennett had firmly established himself as the leading producer of comedies. The Keystones were regarded as the best by audiences, exhibitors, and critics. Sennett had set a new standard by which comic efforts were judged. None rose to his level of achievement.

CHAPTER SIX

Hal Roach and the Rolin "Phunphilms"

THE careers of Hal Roach and Harold Lloyd were bound together inseparably for a number of years. In 1913, Roach, an Elmira, New York, boy who had spent a number of years working in Alaska and the western coastal states, drifted into the San Fernando Valley of California and a job with the Universal unit which was filming J. Warren Kerrigan westerns. Lloyd, originally from Burchard, Nebraska, had attended John Lane Connor's San Diego Dramatic School and had appeared as an extra in an early Edison film starring Ben

Wilson. He came to Hollywood via a traveling stock company which had convinced him that his future was not in drama. His early attempts to find work in films met with no success. Then Harold devised a means of getting by the studio gatekeeper by pretending to be an extra, and once inside, he found work with the Kerrigan unit. It was here that he met Roach.

The two men, both working as extras became friends and were soon spending their spare time discussing the business and how they could better themselves. Roach had several ideas about producing comedies, and Lloyd was still considering the advice which Charlie Ruggles had once given him back in his stock days: "You'll make a much better comedian than an Irving [Sir Henry Irving, of course]." When a new casting director suddenly reduced the pay of all extras from five to three dollars a day, they both quit and parted company. Lloyd was soon employed by the Oz Film Company, which was filming the stories of L. Frank Baum, creator of *The Wizard of Oz*. It was here that the two men met again. Roach had inherited $3,000 and declared his intention of going into the production of film comedies. He offered to hire Lloyd at the three-dollar daily rate. After a few pictures had been made, utilizing varying dress and make-up, Roach and Lloyd finally settled on a character, and "Willie Work" was born.

Wearing a broad-shouldered coat, baggy pants, a tiny hat, and a catlike moustache, Lloyd made several test films which Roach sent to New York but was unable to sell. Just as Roach was approaching the end of his money, Pathé wired an acceptance of *Just Nuts* (April, 1915), with Roy Stewart and Jane Novak as leads. Lloyd had provided the comedy element. The Pathé contract called for all three to work, but Lloyd and Roach had a disagreement over salary and Harold left to join Keystone.

Roach hired Dick Rossen to replace Lloyd, but the venture did not work out. The firm folded and Roach went to Essanay to direct.

Meanwhile, Lloyd's reception on the Keystone lot left something to be desired—in his eyes at least. The Keystone comedians were not impressed by the slender young man, and in their opinion his comedy was neither original nor funny. Lloyd soon began to feel like a small fish in a large pool. When Roach phoned that he had reached an agreement with Pathé for a series of comedies, Harold quit Keystone for Roach's offer of $50.00 a week. Thus the Rolin Film Company went back into business on June 28, 1915, with Gene Marsh as "Mazie Nut" and Clyde and Eleanor Whitney supporting Lloyd in a group of single reels called "Phunphilms."

Back where they had started, Roach and Lloyd made it their first item of business to develop another and more successful characterization. Chaplin had been attracting attention with his costume of oversized clothes. So, in a somewhat unoriginal manner, "Lonesome Luke" evolved as a sort of hayseed copy of Chaplin's character. The idea supposedly came from a creation by TAD (T. A. Dorgan), a popular cartoonist. The baggy trousers became narrow, tight, and short. The coat was cut down from a woman's tailored suit. A too-short vest and small collar were added, along with a very small moustache. Lloyd detested the character but avoided imitating Chaplin's mannerisms, and Pathé was satisfied.

His first release was *Once Every Ten Minutes* (July, 1915) and, by any standards, it was terrible. So, too, was the second, *Spit Ball Sadie,* released two weeks later, in which Harold portrayed a fellow disguised as a female pitcher for a women's baseball team. When his disguise was revealed, he fled. The comedy in it played heavily on the female impersonation and discovery.

It was neither funny nor original and was in fact a bit repugnant at times. The gestures and their meanings were offensive at the time, as, indeed, they would be today. His third film, *Soaking the Clothes* (August, 1915) marked the beginning of more original and tasteful humor.

The "Lonesome Luke" comedies were unenthusiastically greeted by the exhibitors at first, but the fantastic rise in the number of theaters across the nation had created an unbelievable demand for films. And, even after a weak beginning, the "Phunphilms" began to improve in quality. The demand increased, and in February, 1916, Roach announced that the first-run houses in the larger communities were paying twenty-five dollars per booking for a "Lonesome Luke" comedy. Lloyd was still a long way from the great success which would one day come his way; his leading lady, Bebe Daniels, was a teenage beauty also destined to achieve fame, first as Ethel in the Rolin comedies and later with Cecil B. deMille. Harry "Snub" Pollard was hired to support Lloyd and by 1919 had a series of his own.

Typical of the "Lonesome Luke" comedies during this period was *Great While It Lasted* (November, 1915). Bearskin (Lloyd) and Snub were down-and-out for the rent money. Suddenly, from out of nowhere, Bearskin inherited twenty million dollars. With Snub as his butler, Bearskin decided to break into society, but villains stole his trousers, and he was forced to stand in a lake while Snub went home for a barrel. Arriving home together, they discovered that the inheritance had been a mistake, and the money was taken back, leaving the boys where they had started, with no money and all worries.

Business was good enough in July, 1916, for the youthful firm to expand to two units. Lloyd, Gil Pratt, and the original gang continued in one unit, while Harry Todd, Mary Joslin, Fred Newmeyer, Billie Fay, Ben Corday, Fatty Del Hampton, and

Mae White completed the cast of the second. Rolin made a few two-reel comedies which were as good, if not better in many respects, as the single reels, and Lloyd's crew kept up their merry antics with one film a week. In December, 1916, Roach signed a three-year contract calling for the exclusive delivery of all Rolin comedies to Pathé. Pathé was becoming increasingly successful with comedy, and Rolin was its second greatest moneymaker after Pearl White and her serials.

Except for the successful group of early Max Linder films made in France, Pathé had released very little in the way of film humor. At its American studio, only Paul Panzer (later to gain fame in *The Perils of Pauline,* 1914) was making comedies. In *The Cheapest Way* (March, 1913), he had played an Irish father who tricked his daughter (Betty Gray) and her beau (W. J. Williams) into eloping, for the sake of economy. Panzer made several comedies along these lines. Thus the Rolin product helped greatly to balance the Pathé program.

In 1917, Rolin announced the acquisition of Toto, a clown then starring at the Hippodrome. Toto was to join the firm in the fall. Hal Roach was far from challenging Mack Sennett's leadership in screen comedy, but in a short two years he had made remarkable progress toward the top.

Lloyd and Roach continued with the "Lonesome Luke" films through 1916 and most of 1917. Generally their films increased in quality and popularity, but Lloyd was tiring of the Lonesome Luke character. Pathé, however, insisted that he continue his one-a-month double-reel comedies. After all, they were money-makers. After long and seemingly fruitless discussions, Lloyd at last received permission to try another role—provided he continue making the Luke comedies.

The character Lloyd finally chose was the nattily dressed young man with the horn-rimmed glasses that was to make him famous. His breezy personality first appeared on-screen in *Over the Fence* (September, 1917), a one-reel film dealing with baseball. It was an immediate success and now Lloyd had two screen characters—one in double-reel comedies and the other in single reels.

Toto (Arnold Nobello) arrived on the Rolin lot, and Kathleen O'Connor, Clarine Seymour, and Bud Jamison supported him. Roach took over as director of the Toto comedies, leaving Lloyd to direct his own films. *The One Night Stand* was announced as the first Toto release for January 13, 1918, but Roach was not satisfied with it and it was held back for retakes. *The Movie Dummy,* his second film, was released first, and it served to show off to good advantage what the eccentric comic could do. Cast as a worker in a factory which made dummies for the movies, Toto became so discouraged with his job that he longed for escape. Resolving to become a dummy for a day, he filled the bill with himself when an order came in from Rolin. The remainder of the two reels displayed his elasticity, for he was heaved, tugged, and thrown around as if he had no bones at all in his body. Marie Mosquini played the feminine supporting role.

Toto did not complete all of the films for which he had contracted. Not particularly happy with the world of make-believe, he preferred to return to his beloved Hippodrome and the circus tents. On the advice of Alf Goulding, Roach hired another comic, sight unseen, to replace the little clown. So it was that Stan Laurel joined Roach for the first time.

The slight English comedian had been involved with film production before joining Roach. He had arrived in the United States as part of the same Karno troupe that had included Chaplin. When Chaplin left for the movies, the show folded within a month, leaving Laurel without a job. He went into vaudeville and eventually joined Universal, where he worked for Nestor and L-KO in a few undistinguished films. A change in studio personnel resulted in the cancellation of all contracts, but he was able to find work in vaudeville and at Vitagraph, where he worked in a few of Larry Semon's comedies, and from Vitagraph he went to the position with Roach. Laurel made Toto's remaining films for Rolin and then rejoined Vitagraph.[1]

His early films reveal a comic personality quite different from the well-remembered simpleton of the Laurel and Hardy comedies. Stan was a gifted pantomimist, with the ability to improvise. He lived, breathed, and thought in comic terms, and his work of this period was rapid in pace and movement, and full of slapstick, although not much different from the majority of comedians of the time. Neither he nor anyone else imagined what a tremendous future he would have, once teamed with Oliver Hardy.

Hal Roach's most important contribution to screen comedy during this period was the introduction and development of Harold Lloyd. In these years before the twenties, he was busy establishing a company and acquiring comedians and ideas which would find fulfillment at a later date. It was also in the twenties that Roach was to give Sennett his strongest competition, and all of his efforts at this time were directed toward that goal.

[1] *No Place Like Jail, Just Rambling Along, Do You Love Your Wife?, Hustling for Health,* and *Hoot Mon.* Released monthly, beginning in November, 1918, the films were all one reel each. Roach and Frank Terry alternated directing chores.

CHAPTER SEVEN

Comedy and the Independents, 1915–19

B<small>Y</small> 1915 comedy production was striving to meet the demand for new and different material on the screen. The comedy producers operated on a shoestring budget compared with their counterparts in features, and every cent expended had to be strictly accounted for. The cashiers and auditors were reluctant to dip into the bag of production monies. Toward comedy units they were the most penurious of all.

Comedy units had fewer personnel and worked faster than other units. Frank Leon Smith, who worked for Pathé at the time, recalled standing in the door of a Hollywood Boulevard bank one morning: "Along came two autos and parked, dead center in the car tracks. Out jumped cameraman, director, prop men, assistants, and a comedian in an Eskimo suit. With no police to control traffic and, I assume, no warning of any kind to anybody, the lads simply arrived, set up, shot their scenes, packed up and went. I doubt if the entire unit, including performers, consisted of more than five or six individuals."

Mack Sennett made an axiom for comedy producers when he said: "Every three feet of film must pay for itself." At this point in screen history, footage and not time was the measure. When Essanay sent a crew out to film a comedy, a 1,000-foot roll of film was issued to the director. Out of this, he was allowed 20 feet for waste. The remaining 980 feet had to contain the sequences of the completed comedy. Usually, an additional 30 feet were cut out to make room for the titles. If the director used more than this 1,000 feet of raw film to shoot a one-reel comedy, he paid for it out of his own pocket. Comedies had to move and move fast with no interludes between sequences. Each frame of film that rolled over the sprockets had to advance the story if the comedy were to be successful.

When asked about comedy, Fatty Arbuckle had a stock answer: "The plant must come as close as possible to the gag." In a way, this succinctly summed up silent comedy. A package labeled "high explosives" meant that, almost immediately, the comics would begin to tamper with the deadly box. A close-up of a sledge hammer usually augured someone's receiving a friendly tap on the head. Herein was the secret of successful screen comedy—a race-track tempo with gags flying fast and furiously, one pushing its predecessor aside without leaving time for analysis or second thoughts. This made the close coupling of plant and gag an essential rule to follow.

The comedy lots were ramshackle jungles of wooden sheds

and odd-looking structures. Little attention was given to the up-keep of these studios, and many were firetraps. They were used and re-used in scene after scene, and it is a wonder that no disastrous fires ever occurred. In those days, producers gave little thought to safety precautions and staged huge fire scenes indoors, all the while using nitrate film, a highly inflammable material. Whenever a firm did expand its facilities, it was usually to add to already standing structures, but most of the reputed cost had actually been invested in specialized equipment. The permanent buildings were untouched and remained fire hazards.

Comedies of the period (and this remained true to the end of the silent era) inclined toward the vulgar in their content and acting. Arbuckle, Hank Mann, and Sydney Chaplin were three who were perhaps too suggestive in their pictures, but it is difficult to single out these three for criticism when nearly every comedian indulged in this practice. Some of Billy Bevan's antics on the screen in the twenties make one wonder what all the hue and cry over sex is about these days. But audiences seemed to have delighted in these actions and their implications. It is interesting to note that although Chaplin, Lloyd, Semon, Turpin, and to some extent Keaton, indulged in occasional vulgarity early in their careers, little suggestiveness can be found in their later work, which had no need for it.

A number of important developments which took place at this time influenced the future of comedy production. The history of the independent comedy producer—that is, one who did not release through the General Film Company, Universal, or Mutual—did not begin in earnest until late 1914. In October of that year, a group of large exhibitors formed the Kriterion Films Exchange. Under a contract arranged with A. M. Kennedy, general manager of the Mica Film Corporation, Kriterion was supplied with pictures, both dramatic and comedy releases, made by seven small independent producers.[1] The contract guaranteed that only Kriterion would have the right to release their products; in return, each company providing the films was guaranteed the sale of a specific number of copies of each print.

All the studios were located in the burgeoning area around Los Angeles. Each director had been given stock in the firms for which he worked in an attempt to assure that he would do his best work. However, the plan failed, and within nine months Kriterion went bankrupt. S. L. Newman and Lee Sonneborn, two Kriterion exchange men, bought the assets of the distributing company and tried to resurrect the firm. In the meantime, the Associated Film Sales Corporation took over release of many of Kriterion's former suppliers. The entire enterprise folded completely the next year.

United Film Service, another short-lived combination, in 1915 released three series of comedies which enjoyed moderate success. Cameo comedies starred Dan Mason and Harry Kelly, Starlight made the "Heinie and Louie" series with Jimmy Aubrey and Walter Kendig, and Luna displayed the talents of Dot Farley. Aubrey, an English comedian who had worked in the Fred Karno troupe, proved to be quite popular. When United Film Service went out of business,[2] Pathé picked up distribution rights for the Starlight comedies. Aubrey was soon to join Vitagraph. Dot Farley, who had been with Keystone and the St. Louis Motion Picture Company before joining the Albuquerque Film Manufacturing Company, was one of the ugliest little comedians ever to appear on the silent screen. Short and slender, she possessed a small round face and a mouth containing widespread buck teeth, which added to a grotesquely humorous appearance.

[1] Santa Barbara, Thistle, Monty, and Punchinello, Pyramid, Nolege, and Alhambra.
[2] It lasted less than six months, falling into bankruptcy in July, 1915.

With the demise of Kriterion and United, there was little organization in the independent field. Most of the independent producers of the next few years appeared only briefly on the scene and put forth nothing that was above the average. By the middle of 1915, the situation showed signs of improving, but not for long. For the week of June 21–26, there were eighty-six reels issued, of which a full third were comedies.

Another development which became pronounced in 1915 and continued to improve was the animated cartoon. World Film Corporation released a series of one-reelers entitled *The Bert-levyettes,* the work of the popular Bert Levy. Harry Palmer headed a four-man department at Pyramid which turned out the five-hundred-foot Kriterion Komic Kartoon. Palmer moved to Mutual in September to do the *Keeping Up with the Joneses* series. Edison released *The Animated Grouch Chaser,* from the pen of Raoul Barré, a French artist, which utilized live actors as well as drawings.

Two methods of animating characters were commonly used. The most popular—because it was easier—was the "cut-out" method. With this system, the cartoonist used a body with the arms and legs joined to it by pins, moving them slightly as the camera exposed one frame at a time. The final results, however, were jerky and unsatisfactory.

The far superior method, and much more difficult to handle properly, was to trace moving characters on transparent celluloid sheets and superimpose them over water-color backgrounds. Each background could then be used for an entire scene, eliminating the necessity of sketching a new background for each drawing.

Mutt and Jeff were revived in a series placed on the independent market by Harry Grossman's Mutt and Jeff Weekly Company in 1916. Bud Fisher was contracted to do the art work

99

in these three-hundred-foot releases. His cartoons were rapid in action, smoothly executed according to the standards of the time, and without the jumpiness common to many of the animateds. They contained subtitles as well as the dialogue titles within the frames and proved to be very popular. Bud Fisher gained control of the company in May, 1917, instituted a few changes which he felt were needed, and continued to release to the independent market until February, 1918. At that time, he contracted his output to Fox for release, and a steady flow of the split-reel cartoons reached the public in this manner until 1921.

The Katzenjammer Kids, Bringing Up Father, and *Krazy Kat,* coupled with an International News Reel, all appeared together in a split-reel beginning in December, 1916. The Hearst-Vitagraph News Pictorial had earlier in the year featured *Ignatz Mouse* and *Krazy Kat.* Charlie Chaplin became the star of an animated cartoon series state righted[3] by the Herald Film Corporation, which started in February, 1916. These five- to six-hundred-foot reels, however, were never preferred to the genuine article.

The best of the cartoons came from a company headed by J. R. Bray. Attempting to perfect a foolproof method of animating characters in a plausible manner, Bray had begun work in an old farmhouse around 1911. He tried many methods, but none allowed him to produce enough film during a year to cover his expenses. Finally perfecting a process which he jealously guarded and patented, Bray moved into New York City and

[3] Major companies had a system of exchanges which distributed their films to theaters on a rental basis. Independents had no such organized exchanges and relied on independent exchanges or the state-right system. By this system, the independent producer, for a stipulated fee, sold the exclusive territorial rights to exhibit his film in certain states. The purchaser then had the right to distribute the film to exhibitors within this area for whatever price he wished to charge or thought he could get.

established Bray Studio Incorporated with several other men, including Paul Terry, the originator of Farmer Al Falfa.

Bray Studio signed a one-year contract with Paramount in December, 1915, and production began on the *Colonel Heeza Liar* series, which opened with its first release in January, 1916. Combining talents with C. Allan Gilbert, Bray turned out a series of one-reel cartoons for Paramount, using animated drawings and live actors, both in silhouette, with such effectiveness that it was difficult to distinguish between the two. Bobby Bumps and Farmer Al Falfa shared the honors by alternating with Colonel Heeza Liar.

Stage comedians moved over to the movies in large numbers from 1915 on. Neal Burns of the Gayety Musical Stock Company joined Al Christie at Nestor in January. Weber and Fields, Joe Jackson, and Eddie Foy signed with Keystone-Triangle. Victor Moore went to Lasky for a few five-reel features. Kolb and Dill, the German comedians, formed an independent company and made *Glory* for state-right release. W. C. Fields appeared in *The Pool Shark* and *His Lordship's Dilemma* in September for Casino Star comedies. Directed by Edwin Middleton for Gaumont, they were released through Mutual. Fields and Moore were to gain later fame in silent as well as in sound pictures.

The next few years brought many other changes, a number of which worked against the short comedy. Production became costlier and more time-consuming. Whereas Fred Mace had once boasted of shooting a five-hundred-foot comedy in one afternoon, the average two-reel comedy made in 1917 required the expenditure of between twelve and twenty thousand feet of exposed film, to be edited to a release length of approximately two thousand feet.

While the number of theaters in the nation had been constantly increasing, the number of companies producing comedies was diminishing. In fact, by 1919 there was a dearth of good comedies on the market. The influenza epidemic of 1918–19 had closed down a large number of theaters, and the smaller firms were unable to keep their capital invested and still manage to survive. Following Sennett's example, many of the producers radically cut back on production in 1919. He was making only one film a month, instead of six. The Drews, too, were making only one instead of four. Others had reduced their output in a similar manner.

There were many imitators of Charles Chaplin during his most active early years (1914–17), but few of them were as successful as Billy West. West's impersonation was often such that few could tell the difference. In old film clips shown on television in the *Comedy Capers* series or the *Discovery '65* program, viewers may have seen West cavorting on-screen and *assumed* that it was Chaplin. West's close reproduction of Chaplin's character was brisk, alert, and spontaneous, but it lacked the grace and depth of feeling that Chaplin gave his tramp. Also, the Billy West comedies included few close-ups because the deception was much more convincing without them.

To those not especially familiar with Chaplin's work, West's screen appearances may provide some amusement. But to those familiar with the master comedian's genius, West's performances seem superficial and transparent. An easier way to identify one from the other is provided by the character actors who appeared with Chaplin and those who were associated with West. The supporting players in Chaplin's and West's comedies were different, with the single exception of Leo White, who appeared in both men's films. Oliver Hardy played "heavy" for West, as Eric Campbell did for Chaplin.

Born of Jewish parents in Russia, Roy B. Weissberg made his stage debut as William B. West in 1909 at the age of fourteen.

His parents had brought him to America when he was 2½ and he spent his school years in Chicago. From 1909 to 1916, he played vaudeville houses across the country, occasionally picking up extra money as a cartoonist. West's physical stature closely matched Chaplin's. He stood five feet, five inches, weighed 135 pounds, and had brown eyes, black hair, and a dark complexion.

West came to the movies in 1916 via a contract with the Unicorn Film Service, an independent distribution organization headed by Ike Schlank. Unicorn signed Billy for a series of double reels, and he was to be supported by Ethelyn Gibson and Howard Messmore. Miss Gibson was an Akron girl who had made her stage debut in 1914; Unicorn was her movie debut. Edwin McKim directed. Three comedies were completed when Unicorn failed financially, and West's contract was turned over to the Belmont Film Company, another independent formed in an effort to salvage something from Unicorn's collapse. Fritz Wintermeyer (or Wintermeier), who claimed to have directed Chaplin at Essanay, put West in one more two-reel comedy before Belmont, too, succumbed.

West then signed a five-year contract with the Caws Comedy Corporation for a salary of $750.00 weekly. His contract called for two single-reel comedies a month, to be distributed on a state-right basis. For reasons unknown, the Caws Comedy Corporation changed its name to King Bee before production began. Louis Burstein was president and general manager, L. L. Hiller served as treasurer, and Nat H. Spitzer was sales manager. Arthur M. Werner, Charles Abrams, and Sam Cummins were other prominent people at Caws who carried over to King Bee. As a lawyer, Burstein had been instrumental in the founding of both the New York Motion Picture Company and Keystone. He left the industry in 1914, but returned as the backbone of the Wizard Film Company, which introduced Burns and Stull

(Pokes and Jabbs) to the world of comedy films. A short-lived company, Wizard was absorbed by the Equitable Film Corporation, and Burstein then formed Vim.

Arvid E. Gillstrom was hired as director of the Billy West comedies. Gillstrom was a native of Gothenburg, Sweden. He claimed to have been a mining engineer, prospector, and soldier of fortune, and made his movie debut as an acrobat and high diver. A former director for Mack Sennett, he traded heavily on this reputation, purporting to have been Chaplin's director at Keystone. If there is a shred of truth to his claim of having worked with Chaplin, it is only as an assistant to Henry Lehrman on the first few Chaplin Keystones. Note that once they became associated with West, both Wintermeyer and Gillstrom claimed to have been responsible for Chaplin's success.

Production started in Jacksonville, Florida, with Herman Obrock as cameraman and Ben H. Cohen as chief editor. Oliver Hardy, Ethel Burton, Leo White, Florence McLaughlin, Polly Van, Joe Cohen, Bud Ross, and Ethelyn Gibson made up the supporting cast. Rosemary Theby and Myrtle Lind joined the ranks later. Having married Gillstrom in the spring of 1917, Miss Burton appeared as the lead in the first four West comedies. She left King Bee but returned in 1918 and resumed her former role as leading lady with *The Rogue*. Before the King Bee series was finished, Charles Parrott took Gillstrom's place as director. (Charles Parrott was just as successful on-screen as he was off. His screen alias was Charlie Chase.)

The first three comedies were shown privately at the New Albany Theater in Brooklyn during late April, 1917. The first one went into official release on May 15, to be followed by a new double-reel comedy every second week. During this time, West was being sued by his former employers. They sought to prevent him from appearing in any pictures except those he had previously made, claiming that his contract was still valid. The suit was dismissed on the grounds that the contract was no longer valid or binding.

After finishing the fifth comedy, the entire company left Jacksonville for New York City. The next film was shot at the Frohman studio in Flushing, Long Island, and then the King Bee players moved to Bayonne, New Jersey, to use studio facilities formerly operated by Vim.

The Bee Hive Exchange was established to handle the state rights for New York and New Jersey. By October 1, it announced that more than four hundred exhibitors in the area were showing Billy West comedies. Bee Hive also claimed an expedition of $3,000 weekly in advertising under the direction of Ed Rosenbaum, the publicity head of King Bee.

Ellen Burford signed a one-year contract in October, 1917. Great things were expected of this petite twenty-four-year-old beauty from Louisville. Leatrice Joy and Helen Spencer also joined the company. Miss Spencer came directly from Vitagraph's "O. Henry" series. Oliver Hardy, too, signed a new contract, but one that had a twist. Hardy weighed 265 pounds at the time. Burstein apparently felt that an additional 50 pounds would be desirable, and Hardy's contract called for an extra two dollars for every pound gained. If he gained the entire 50 pounds within six months, Hardy received a $250 bonus. However, history fails to record the outcome.

Having completed a backlog of comedies while in Bayonne, the King Bee troupe on October 22, 1917, boarded a fast express bound for Los Angeles. They arrived on the twenty-fourth and went directly to the Christie studio, which Burstein had arranged to lease. Christie's new studio was nearing completion, and he was glad to put the older facilities in use for a profit.

As a publicity stunt, King Bee insured West for $50,000. This insurance was to be valid for the duration of West's five-year contract. Rex Taylor and Bud Ross were busily drafting scripts when Burstein announced that King Bee would soon star West in a five-reel feature comedy. This super-spectacular was to be entitled *King Solomon,* or perhaps even *Ol' King Sol,* and was scheduled for release in early 1918. Meanwhile, production began on the first King Bee comedy to be made in California, *The Slave.* This picture marked the initial appearance of Leatrice Joy as West's leading lady. It was also highly touted as the first comedy containing no subtitles whatsoever to help carry the story. Reviewers found this lack of subtitles did not affect the story, and *The Slave* was considered a great success.

In an ironic turn of events, the Chaplinesque West was himself about to face competition from an imitator. In the fall of 1917, two King Bee exectives stopped over in Boston to catch the act of vaudeville comic Ray Hughes, whom they liked so well that they bowed out of the company to form their own production unit with him. Arthur Werner and Charles Abrams established Pyramid and invited Harry Palmer to sit on the executive board. William A. Seiter was hired as producer-director, and Harry L. Reichenbach, an expert public relations agent, took over direction of the advertising and exploitation. The eccentric comedian Hughes was signed for five years, and Pyramid, planning to move to Hollywood later, began production at Fort Lee, New Jersey. Abrams and Werner hoped to duplicate the success that King Bee had enjoyed with West.

The Pyramid product was announced to the trade in December, 1917. Four comedies had been completed and the advertising campaign launched. The stated policy was to make twenty-four double-reel comedies a year. Further comedies were to be made, but since Pyramid had not settled on a definite method of distribution by March, 1918, it became clear that the fledgling company would probably not become a major challenge. Finances necessary to keep the company afloat were obtained by selling foreign rights to the completed pictures. The money thus obtained was expended in production of two additional comedies before Pyramid faded from the scene. Director Seiter went over to Jester in June, 1918.

Several changes took place in the King Bee organization during April, 1918. Burstein indefinitely postponed the projected five-reel feature for West without giving any specific reason. Charles Parrott had become director-general on April 1, replacing Gillstrom, who joined Fox. Fay Holderness was added to the players' roster. The move which held the greatest importance for the future was made by a salesman of silk ribbons, Milton L. Cohen, who bought the original Bee Hive Exchange and showed an active interest in King Bee.

An interesting sidelight is provided by the statistical data released by King Bee's publicity department. In its first year King Bee, according to the department, hired 1,400 actors and actresses to take part in twenty comedies. About 170,000 feet of film had been shot to make the necessary 40,000 feet of negatives. And the company had expended about 1,400 pies, 3,621 quarts of mush, 1,322 buckets of soap suds, and 300 barrels of flour.

Billy West's King Bee comedies came to an end with *Play-mates*. West appeared in this one without his moustache, as he and Hardy played two kids in rompers. Although announcement was made of *Beauties in Distress*, it does not appear to have been completed or released. The company's star was scheduled for a two-week vacation beginning July 1, 1918, and here the story lapses. It may be that King Bee had overextended itself financially. Burstein formed another company under the name

Burston and signed Francis Ford for serial production. Nothing else was heard from Billy West until the end of the year, although he did work in 3 pictures at Vitagraph.

In December, 1918, Milton Cohen announced the formation of the Bull's Eye Film Corporation, and Nat Spitzer became studio manager. After recovering from a bout with influenza, West was re-engaged. Leo White and Stanton P. Heck signed on as the "heavies." Ethelyn Gibson returned to play the female leads. Charles Parrott had been directing comedies at L-KO, but dropped everything to work once more with West. Parrott directed all of the new West comedies and even wrote many of them himself, although Vincent Bryon had been hired to do the scripts. Production began at 1329 Gordon Street in Hollywood (the former home of King Bee), and on December 15, the first Bull's Eye comedy was released to the independent market under the title, *He's In Again*. Mack Swain soon replaced Stanton Heck as West's foil. A new series starring Gale Henry was also planned, but influenza kept Miss Henry off the screen until May, 1919, when *A Wild Woman* appeared as her first release.

William Parsons, the president of the National Film Corporation, came out from behind his desk and went before the camera as "Smiling Bill" Parsons in late 1918. His films were released on the independent market as Capitol Comedies and were successful enough to be picked up by Goldwyn for trade release in 1919. Capitol expanded in that year and acquired Carter De Haven, who had made a two-reel series for Universal in 1916, *Timothy Dobbs, That's Me*. De Haven went to work and turned out a group of thirteen films, beginning with *In a Pinch* (May, 1919). His comedy style was in the same vein as the late Sidney Drew's, and he found favor with exhibitors and fans alike.

In 1916 the Fox Film Company, in order to present a well-balanced program, decided that the time had arrived for its first short comedy production. A unit was established under the direction of Charles Parrott (Charlie Chase), with Hank Mann and Lee Morris as stars. Fox also engaged Henry Lehrman, who had left L-KO, and his unit included Billie Ritchie and Dot Farley. Walter C. Reed and Harry Edwards were added to the staff of directors, and Charles Arling, "Smiling Billy" Mason, Amy Jerome, Annette DeFoe, Joe Lee, and Anna Luther completed the players.

Fox was able to announce to the trade in December, 1916, that production had begun on the Foxfilm comedies, with the first release due on January 1, 1917. This was *Social Pirates,* with Arling in the lead. Fox's statement included the fact, that fifty-two comedies in two reels would be produced in 1917. The company name was unexpectedly changed to Sunshine Comedies in March, but shortly reverted to Foxfilms.

The Fox program often led to confusion from these many changes during its first year of existence. In June the comedy schedule was split into two divisions—Foxfilms and Sunshines. The former were made by units under the direction of Mann, Parrott, and Tom Mix, whose early pictures for Fox definitely contained comedy elements. The Sunshine group was further split into thirds under the over-all supervision of Lehrman, who also directed a unit. David Kirkland and Jay Howe handled the other two.

The Fox comedy ranks swelled quickly with Mae Busch and Ford Sterling from Keystone-Triangle, Paddy McGuire from Vogue, Lloyd Hamilton from Kalem, and Charles "Heine" Conklin. Lehrman's Sunshine organization did not begin actual operation until October, 1918, and its first release, *Roaring Lions and Wedding Bells,* came in November.

Paramount, the distributor for Zukor's Famous Players and

Lasky's Feature Play Company, moved to balance its release schedule in 1916. Victor Moore had made a few feature comedies in 1915, but they were not enough to balance the Paramount program. Short films were needed, and the U. S. Motion Picture Company was established to produce the one-reel Black Diamond comedies, beginning in October.

Klever Komedies made their appearance in December with *The Best Man*. Starring Victor Moore—this time in one-reelers— the Klever Komedies were quite good. Moore, well known in vaudeville circles, did a fine group of films which portrayed the difficulties encountered by the average married man. The plots were simple, as is illustrated by some of the titles—*Bungalowing* (June, 1917), *Commuting* (June, 1917), *Moving* (May, 1917), and *Flivvering* (March, 1917). In each film, Moore built the comic action around the single topic in such a way that he got many laughs.

The big news at Paramount was the acquisition of Roscoe Arbuckle, who had signed a contract with Joseph M. Schenck at the end of 1916. The Comique Film Corporation was established with studios in New York City, and Arbuckle left California in January, 1917. He was to begin production by March 1, if possible, and he gathered a group of players including Al St. John, Alice Lake, Charles Dudley, and Josephine Stevens before going to work on his first release, *The Butcher Boy* (April, 1917).

Arbuckle's Comique films were excellent in story line, action, and humor. His idea of comedy production was to keep things moving and thus avoid the risk of losing the audience. Speed, or fast pacing within the film, was the essence of Arbuckle's comedy. When he began a picture, he did his best to keep everyone keyed to a high pitch, feeling that players did their best work under such conditions.

It is to Arbuckle's credit that the vulgarity found in his Keystone films did not creep into his Comique pictures, at least not to any great degree. His short comedies were welcomed with enthusiasm by exhibitors everywhere. Everyone seemed to want them, and Paramount found it necessary to place two hundred prints in circulation instead of the seventy-five which it had thought sufficient. Continued success with the shorts led Arbuckle into an ambitious feature program, which was cut short by his involvement in a notorious incident at a party, which provoked a scandal and led to his being tried for manslaughter.[4]

Although he was finally acquitted by a jury after three trials, his career was ruined forever. Several films which had been completed were allowed to gather dust in the vaults, for they had no market value. He found that work in the movies was nearly impossible to get, for he had been thrown to the wolves by the frightened industry that he had done so much to help develop. Perhaps no other business in the nation could have disposed of one of its members as quickly and effectively as did the motion pictures. Through the friendship of a few who stood by him, Arbuckle tried his hand at directing features in the late twenties, but he worked with little enthusiasm. A contract to direct and star in a group of four comedy shorts for Warner Brothers in 1933 did occupy him for a time and he was very happy while making them, for he felt it was an opportunity for a comeback. Shortly after finishing them, he succumbed to a heart attack and died at the age of forty-six on June 29, 1933.

In view of the fate that had overtaken this funny fat man, it is ironic to recall that he had once remarked: "I shall produce nothing that will offend the proprieties, whether applied to children or grown-ups. My pictures are turned out with clean hands

[4] For accounts of the trial, its background and outcome, see Buster Keaton and Charles Samuels, *My Wonderful World of Slapstick* and Terry Ramsaye, *A Million and One Nights.*

and, therefore, with a clear conscience which, like virtue, is its own reward. Nothing would grieve me more than to have mothers say, 'Let's not go there today, Arbuckle is playing and he isn't fit for the children to see.' I want them to always speak otherwise of me, for as long as I can please the kiddies, I don't care who entertains their elders."

Even though the comedy factories were grinding out their products as fast as they could, such a market existed for humor on the screen that a group of independent firms were formed to exploit the reissue of earlier comedies. W. H. Productions and the Jans Producing Corporation both re-released Keystones of 1914 vintage, along with the early "Ham and Bud" films. The Tower Film Corporation re-released a number of Keystones and a separate set of the Arbuckle Keystone comedies. Even Fox reissued its first thirteen Sunshines to the exhibitors from June through August, 1919, as "The Lucky Thirteen."

Frohman Amusement Corporation grandly announced the signing of Mack Swain and Lotty Cruze for a group of one-reel films to be known as Poppy Comedies. They began with *Ambrose's Day Off* (May, 1919). Swain relied on the character which had won his popularity while he was in the Sennett ranks, but the enthusiasm died out quickly, for the films did not live up to audience expectations. The General Film Company officially expired this same year, bringing to an end the remainder of a trust which had dominated the early days of the motion picture (the Motion Picture Patents Company was dissolved about two years earlier).

As this formative period of screen comedy drew to a close, it was clear that there remained little in sight which was new. Comedy situations and their variations—and variations on the variations—had been used and reused hundreds of times. All of which finally amounted to one thing: the successful screen comedian of the next decade was to be the one whose *style* was the variation. Enlightened producers realized that the basic store-house of comic ideas had long been exhausted. Thus the refreshing breeze in the comedy of the twenties was to be the comedian's own personality. The ranks of screen comedians were thinned in the twenties. Those without enough talent to support their material fell by the wayside. The major comics, after all, were *personalities* who owed their success not so much to their material as to what they were able to do with it. This ability to rise above the script elevated several comedians to a place far above their contemporaries.

CHAPTER EIGHT

The Twenties

THE year 1920 can well be considered a high point in the history of visual comedy. Several factors made the twenties "The Golden Age of Comedy." European, and especially English, production of short comedies had been set back sharply by World War I, allowing the American film to move into foreign markets with increasing vigor and thus effecting an American monopoly in some senses of the word. Competition within the American market was a definite trait of the period and became more and more characteristic as the twenties rolled on, furiously heading for the era of sound. Independent producers in increasing numbers tried their luck in the movies, but many went out of business almost as fast as they went in. The Hollywood producers did not feel that it was their responsibility to educate or enlighten—the money was in entertaining the public, and entertainment was just what they provided.

By the beginning of the twenties, the feature film of five or more reels had long been the accepted industry standard. Most houses changed their bill twice a week, and short comedies, along with a newsreel and novelty or travelogue, were required for each change and used as fillers. During the 1927–28 season, nineteen distributors announced a total schedule of 1,912 releases, of which 607—or nearly one-third—were comedy shorts. This was markedly different from the early years, especially the prewar era.

By 1928 short comedy production had caught up with the demand. Whereas in earlier days each producer had been hard at work the year round, Educational, Universal, Christie, Warners, and Sennett now closed down their comedy units from February through May, having already completed the season's filming. Longer feature films were the rule, and many of these were light comedies, which eliminated the practice of adding a comedy short to the bill. This meant in effect that the demand for the shorter product was not nearly as great as it had been in earlier years, and most of the independent firms had gone out of business by this time. Nineteen twenty-seven was to mark the beginning of the sound era, and all of the short-subject producers were releasing some films with at least a synchronized score. Hal Roach and Mack Sennett were doing this in 1928. The following season was to see Al Christie convert to the Movietone process.

The beginning of the twenties was the heyday for many comedy producers. By 1920–21 Mutual and General Film had passed from the scene; most of the pioneer firms were out of business. Their place had been taken over by the Educational Film Corporation of America, established by Earl Hammons in 1919 to make educational pictures for schools and churches. Although Hammons soon discovered that little demand existed for his original idea, he continued with it. However, he also entered the field of theatrical distribution in 1920 with the Educational Film Exchange, using the system he had built up as a release unit for Mermaid, Chester, Christie, and Torchy comedies.

Mermaid was founded by Jack White and Lloyd Hamilton to exploit the latter's talents. White became one of the more prolific comedy directors of the period. Lige Conley signed for the 1921–22 season, and Mermaid was on its way. Next to Hamilton, the company's best comedian was Jimmy Adams, a sort of poor man's Charlie Chase. Adams was slight and shorter than Chase, and he used similar mannerisms even though his comedy had more slapstick.

The Torchy comedies began as a starring vehicle for Johnny Hines, who had been in films since 1915. C. C. Burr, hoping to become a leading independent producer during the period, founded Master Films and acquired Hines from the World Film Corporation to play the red-headed office boy made popular by the stories of Sewell Ford. Dorothy Mackaill, a seventeen-year-old English girl who had played the London Hippodrome and who had arrived in this country as a member of the Ziegfeld Midnight Frolic, was given the female lead. Burr arranged for distribution under the Educational banner, and *Torchy* hit the nation's funny bone on July 11, 1920. This started a long series of two-reel comedies which eventually led Hines into feature comedies.

Al Christie, who left the independent field to release through

Educational, utilized the services of Neal Burns, Bobby Vernon, and Fay Tincher, among others, during this time. He continued to turn out the polite comedies with a dash of slapstick which had made him famous. Over the years Christie built several new studios from his earnings. After Sennett and Roach, he was one of filmdom's most popular funmakers. One of the big dramatic hits of 1922 was Valentino's *The Sheik*. Sennett burlesqued it with *The Shreik of Araby*. So did Christie, with *That Son of a Sheik*, a September release featuring Neal Burns.

The Arrow Film Corporation, one of the leading independents, entered the comedy field with considerable fanfare. Hank Mann signed for twenty-six two-reel films in 1920. The team of Lyons and Moran broke up. Moran remained at Universal and Lyons joined Arrow, where he starred in a series and also supervised Bobby Dunn in the Mirthquake comedies. C. B. C. Film Sales Corporation released Carnival's comedies with Polly Moran and "Smiling Bill" Jones in 1921–22. Federated Film Exchange put forth the "Hallroom Boys" comedies, produced by the Cohn brothers, who were later to gain recognition at Columbia. Sidney Smith and Harry McCoy starred in these double reels, but Jimmy Adams left Mermaid to replace McCoy late in 1921. Adams returned to Mermaid the following August.

Federated also released the "Monte Banks" series, made by Warner Brothers, which proved to be very popular. Banks (né Bianchi) was an Italian boy who came to the United States at seventeen and had first appeared in Universal's comedies. A suave little fellow with a dapper moustache, Banks graduated to a long series with Grand-Asher Distributing Corporation before going on his own to produce feature comedies for Pathé in the later twenties. Milburne Moranti and Helen Williams also made a series of one-reel comedies for Federated release.

After recovering from an attempt to commit suicide, Billy

Quirk turned up in 1921 to do his last series of films. These were made for Reelcraft, an independent company formed in 1920 by combining the holdings of the Bull's Eye Film Corporation, the Emerald Motion Picture Company, and Interstate Film of New York. "Smiling Billy" Mason attempted a comeback in two-reel comedies in 1922 after a long interval on the vaudeville stage, but he did not succeed. Like many of the comics who were popular in the early days, Mason had not developed new ideas in his comedy, and he lost his popularity with audiences. To be successful in an independently produced comedy series, the comedian usually had to be better than his material. The independent producers were not generally noted for their story lines or their production values, and their films were in fact often the poorest in the comedy field. For comedians not accepted by the producer-distributors and for those on their way down from success, the independent field became a graveyard, a sort of final resting place before oblivion.

Billy West reappeared in a 1921 series for the Joan Film Sales Company, another independent. He had once been one of the most successful comics in state-right releases, and his first film for Joan, *Sweethearts,* came as a big surprise—West had dropped his imitation of Chaplin. From 1922 to 1926, Billy made a continuous series of light and polite comedies for Arrow, then went on to megaphone comedies for Fox in 1927.

Comedies were in such demand in the early part of the decade that Hunt Stromberg, an independent producer, was able to announce a contract with Metro in 1922. He was to produce, over a two-year span, a series of eight comedies starring the inimitable Bull Montana, a well-known athlete. The first of the group, *A Ladies' Man,* was a three-reeler issued in October. The ungainly Montana was a scream in a tuxedo, and he had no trouble finding regular work in pictures after this series expired.

The Fox program picked up steam in 1920 when Clyde Cook, the principal clown and pantomimist at the Hippodrome, was signed. Cook opened in December with *Don't Tickle.* The wiry little Australian comedian was an extremely talented acrobat, and he soon gained the nickname, "The Kangaroo Boy." Chester Conklin had come to Fox from Sennett and began his films with *Chicken á la Cabaret* in January. The most talented comic on the lot was Lupino Lane, a versatile acrobat and tumbler. A well-known member of a renowned family of acrobats who had emigrated from Italy to England in the eighteenth century, Lane had previously made comedies in England and was no stranger to screen methods.

He made his American debut on Broadway in September, 1920, with the English production *Afgar.* A film contract had been signed in October, 1921, but stage commitments did not allow Lane to join Fox immediately. After the New York run of *Afgar* closed, Lupino went on the road with the touring company until the end of 1921. His first film for Fox, *The Broker* (March, 1922), was not particularly effective, but by the time his second series opened with *The Reporter* in August, he had found more suitable material. In this film he played a newspaperman covering a revolution in Mexico. After various comic mishaps, he finally concluded that it was safer to read about revolutions than to cover them. Lane was a comedian who was better than his material. By the late twenties, he was turning out some excellent footage for Educational release.

When the 1922–23 season began, Fox was in high gear with six comedy series on the market. Besides Cook and Lane, there was Al St. John, the Lee Kids, Mutt and Jeff (still in split reels), and the Sunshine comedies, which used various comedians. Fox had prospered, and it would soon reach its peak, then decline before the decade ended.

Al St. John's material was also improving. *All Wet* (September, 1922) was the story of a newly married couple and a quack real estate agent. Al's reaction to the agent's "proof" that the soil was fertile by the miraculous growth of corn and melons was a comic highlight in the film.

Vitagraph still had Larry Semon and Jimmy Aubrey, but Albert E. Smith was trying desperately to compete in the feature field, and his comedy program suffered as a result. Aubrey left Vitagraph in 1924 to do a series for Standard Cinema, which released through Selznick. Paramount's major comedy releases were made by the Carter De Havens, who began a series of ten two-reelers with *Hoodooed* (February, 1920). De Haven and his wife, Flora Parker, then left Paramount to make several features for First National before joining the R-C Pictures Corporation, which in 1923 released through the Film Booking Office. Here De Haven began a series which followed the trials of a newly married couple. He opened in September with *Their First Vacation*, the story of a new bridegroom's fruitless search for a quiet and peaceful honeymoon spot.

By 1924, Educational was releasing comedy series with Walter Hiers, Lige Conley, Jack McHugh, Jimmy Adams, Neal Burns, and Al St. John. St. John's comedies were by far the most popular, not so much from what he did as how he did it. In *Stupid, but Brave* (September, 1924), Al had to cross the country by a specified date in order to take advantage of a job offer, but was without funds for the trip. In the course of events, he came across a group of escaped convicts who stripped him of his clothes and left their prison garb behind. Realizing the consequences of wearing such apparel, Al preferred his BVD's, and many laughs resulted as he made his way down the road so attired. When a group of runners came along, Al joined the race.

He managed to win, grabbed the prize money, and shot off down the road once again with the sheriff right behind him.

The Fox comedy program did not stay very long at the top. In 1925, Fox was making only two brands of comedies, Imperial and Sunshine. Their all-star casts had long departed, and Arthur Houseman was the only successful comic left on the lot. In 1928, Fox released only twenty-six comedy shorts and eight of these featured animals. Fox had discovered that it took an increasing amount of ingenuity and money to produce comedies which could compete favorably in the market. The company chose not to remain comedy-oriented, preferring instead to allow its theaters to book shorts from elsewhere in the late twenties.

Universal's comedy program throughout the mid-twenties was in about the same class as the Fox schedule. Quality and quantity had slipped from the position once attained by the Al Christie and Lyons-Moran team. Standard plots featuring minor comics were used, and the results which were put on the market were discouraging for exhibitors. There were some comedies clever in concept and execution, but for a firm as large and diversified as Universal, the proportion of these seemed insignificant. Universal, of all the major motion picture producers, remained for a long time the closest to an assembly-line factory. By 1925, it was turning out only Blue Bird (with Al Alt) and Century comedies, the latter relying mostly on animals. In the true sense of the word, Universal comedies were only fillers.

It was not until 1926 that Universal's comedy program began to show some interesting developments. The Stern brothers took over as producers of a majority of the short subjects and began the *What Happened To Jane* series with Thelma Daniels, Max Asher, and Charles King. Scott Pembroke directed these welcome additions to the scene. Production under the Sterns was rapid, and even though not much attention was given to the material used, much of it was in the same vein as Al Christie's —polite humor with a dash of slapstick. Like so many other producers, the Sterns were in business for the fast dollar, but they were lucky enough to hit upon a winning formula which audiences liked.

The formula was successfully duplicated again in 1926 with *The Newlyweds and Their Baby* series. Ethlyne Clair was cast as Mrs. Newlywed in these comedies, which were adapted from the cartoons of George McManus. Gus Meins and Francis Corby shared the director's duties. Sunny McKeen, who at the age of eighteen months gave his first "performance" as Baby Snookums in the "Newlywed" comedies, was so popular that he was put in a series of his own. By the he time he was four, he was making more than $15,000 a year from his screen "work." The comedies were done in much the same vein as the "Smith Family" series which Sennett was releasing.

Another comic worth mentioning from the Universal program of this time is skinny Syd Saylor, whose comedy trademark was a bobbing Adam's apple. A breezy and likable screen personality, Saylor joined the Stern brothers in 1927 and stayed till the end of the silents.

There was one other group of Universal shorts which helped fill the demand for comedy releases. This was the two-reel Junior Jewels released under the title of *The Collegians*. This series began in 1926 with *Benson at Calford* and followed the exploits of a country boy who was awarded a university scholarship as the result of winning a foot race. In these comedy-dramas, he was introduced to the different aspects of college life. The series lasted through 1929 and Benson's graduation.

George Lewis played the lead in these refreshing vignettes of young manhood, supported by Dorothy Gulliver as the sweetheart who was also the dean's daughter. Edward Phillips was the smart-alecky "big man on campus," who usually got taken down a peg or two by the end of the second reel, only to reappear in the next film as cocky as ever. Harry Edwards, Robert F. Hill, Wesley Ruggles, Nat Ross, Ben Holmes, and Harry Fraser all took turns at directing.

Lupino Lane joined Educational in 1925 for a series which lasted until 1929. Lane was still the rubber-jointed champion of acrobatics, and he did several comedies which have never received proper attention. One such film was *Monty of the Mounted* (August, 1927), a fine burlesque on the old Northwest Mounted Police theme. Lane's unusual ability as a comedy tumbler and all-around gymnast was used to good advantage.

As the rookie, Lupino was the only Mountie left who had not gone after Black Pete and failed to get his man. The honor of the force was at stake, and even though the Sergeant hated to do it, he sent for his last man. Eager to prove himself, Monty fell all over the Sergeant while trying to assume a military bearing. After Lane had left to carry out his assignment, the Sergeant revealed that the wanted criminal was in fact his own twin brother, and he decided that only he could do the job properly. Changing into backwoods garb, he headed out in pursuit of Monty and Black Pete.

In the meantime, Monty was having troubles with his recalcitrant horse (actually a cleverly constructed and surprisingly realistic dummy), which he could not get to stand up on all fours. Finally, in town, Monty was warned by the tavern keeper's daughter that Black Pete would kill him, but he rode over to the tavern to make the arrest anyway. Confronted by Pete's men, Monty went through all sorts of slips, slides, and falls. The funniest moment came as Monty put on his overcoat, held for him by one of the crooks. With his arm in one sleeve, Monty turned and somehow entangled the crook in the other coat sleeve. When Monty pulled out a cigaret, the crook lit it. After Monty took a puff, the other arm removed the cigaret from his mouth, reversed it, and reinserted it.

The arrival of Black Pete and the Sergeant was the cue for more confusion. After a furious fight, Monty discovered that he had hog-tied and handcuffed the Sergeant, whom he thought to be Black Pete, only to look out of the window to see the villain riding away with the tavern keeper's daughter. A wild chase on horseback ensued. Black Pete was finally caught by Monty with a rope trick, and the tavern keeper's daughter was saved, thus bringing the film to a successful conclusion.

Lane was an extremely youthful-looking comedian, whose one expression was that of an empty-headed child. In this respect he sometimes resembled Harry Langdon. Lane's talents as an acrobat cannot be exaggerated, for he was the best. But as interesting as his acrobatic work was, and even though his comedies was popular at the time, Lane was never really able to bridge the gap between success and greatness.

Wallace Lupino, Lupino Lane's brother, was an interesting comedian in his own right, and he starred in a series of Cameo comedies, also released by Educational. These were more of the polite domestic comedies, which depended mostly upon the situations for their laughs, rather than the comic ability of the actors.

Al Christie was still making money from his comedies, and he built a new thirty-acre studio in 1927–28. His program for the previous season had consisted of thirty two-reel comedies: eight with Bobby Vernon, six with Jimmy Adams, ten with Neal Burns, and six with Billy Dooley, a one-time supporting comic now raised to stardom. Dooley used a sailor suit for his comic costume, and there was more than a passing resemblance to Larry Semon in his dim-witted actions and appearance.

Paramount acquired the Christie comedies for release in 1927–28, and Vernon, Adams, and Dooley each made eight. Another twelve were produced with Burns, Jack Duffy, and Anne Cornwall. These comedies were dignified enough to accompany the Paramount features, and Christie's releases remained there.

Al Herman and J. A. Duffy directed the "Mickey McGuire" comedies, produced first by R-C Pictures Corporation and then by Standard Cinema for Film Booking Office release. The popular series was created from the cartoons by Fontaine Fox and starred young Joe Yule, Jr. as Mickey, the tough little main character. A favorite with young and old alike, Yule had entered pictures with roles in Colleen Moore's First National features and worked the series profitably into the early years of sound. He gained greater fame some years later at Metro-Goldwyn-Mayer as Mickey Rooney.

The art of animation was well developed by the twenties, and the cartoon producers were kept busy. Bray Productions put Walter Lantz at work with a weekly release, which usually featured Dinky Doodle. Colonel Heeza Liar was revived and sent back to the screen. From 1925 through 1928, Pat Sullivan placed Felix the Cat on theater bills, courtesy of Educational. The most famous of the cartoons were made by Paul Terry, who had left Bray shortly after the firm was founded. His work was released through Pathé, and his Aesop Fables were common screen fare throughout the period.

Viewing the cartoons today, one is struck by two things. The unpolished artwork of these black-and-white cartoons differs little from the Terrytoons of the thirties and forties. It is also comparable to the cartoons that Terry made for Official Films, which are still playing on television today. The other striking aspect of Terry's work in the twenties is found in the dominance of violence. Of course, violence in cartoons has long been accepted, and even the best made by Hollywood have thrived on it. Nearly everyone is familiar with the "Tom and Jerry" series made in the forties and early fifties in which poor Tom often lost his teeth and was flattened at least once in every reel. However, the violence was all for the sake of fun, and it was presented as fantasy. After Tom was flattened by a steam roller, he would spring back to life, no worse for wear. The bomb which exploded and stripped him of his fur amounted to no real harm, for the fur miraculously reappeared in the following scene as if nothing had happened and with no portrayal of agony.

In Terry's Aesop Fables, violence was used for its own sake. *Do Women Pay* (November, 1923) was the story of two mice and a cat. The cat, portrayed as being extremely vicious, kidnapped the lady mouse, carrying her off to his hideout, where he set forth champagne. Her refusal to drink a toast enraged the cat, who began chasing her. The boy mouse, flying to the rescue on a stork, parachuted into the chimney. Popping out of the stove just as the cat had cornered his love, the mouse drew a pistol and shot. The cartoon showed the bullet clearly as it traveled through the air and lodged in the cat's body. Blood gushed forth, and the cat staggered around in agony, finally falling to the floor, where he died with the blood still flowing. The "happy" ending had the two mice embracing by the body of the dead villain.

Walt Disney came on the cartoon scene in 1926, doing a series of Alice cartoons for Winkler Pictures with release through R-C Pictures. Disney tried to combine human figures with animated characters in these cartoons, with limited success. Forming his own company, he landed a contract with Universal for a group of Oswald Rabbit cartoons. Reasonably successful, the cartoons pleased Universal, but Disney felt that they could be improved and went to New York City to persuade his distributor to allow him to expand his production methods. This suggestion was not greeted with favor by Universal executives, who realized that higher production costs would cut into their profit margin. Disney remained adamant and lost his contract as a result.

On the return trip to California, Disney conceived the idea for Mortimer Mouse, soon to revolutionize the cartoon world. Finishing the Oswald cartoons which completed his Universal contract, Walt set to work and filmed his first mouse cartoon, sending it to New York in an attempt to arrange distribution. However, it was greeted as just another of the silent cartoons, which by 1928 were considered passé. Sound had become the thing in the cartoon field, so Walt withdrew *Steamboat Willie* as a silent cartoon and took it to New York, where he was able to add the sound score just as he wanted it. Offers to buy him out were made, but all Disney wanted to sell was his product. Independent release seemed to be the only alternative. This mouse cartoon, with the sound added, was an immediate hit with the public, who had never seen a musical cartoon before. Disney had experienced the most difficult part of his career. The rest, as they say, is history.

CHAPTER NINE

Silver Screen and Golden Comedy

HAL Roach's comedy factory
expanded constantly during the twenties. Harry "Snub" Pollard
had been given his own series of single reels beginning with
Start Something in October, 1919, and Eddie Boland came in
1920 to star in several one-reelers. Roach found himself without
enough space to accommodate his increased output and added
another 100-by-200-foot enclosed stage early in 1921. This addition allowed him to double his production beginning on March
1. As part of this program, he tried to revive the "Lonesome
Luke" character by using Harold Lloyd's brother, Gaylord, but

the attempt was unsuccessful. Comics were difficult to get at this time; all of the good ones were working. To meet the demand for comedies, Roach selected a group of the more successful single reels which Harold Lloyd had made in 1916–18 and reissued them to the trade.

Harold Lloyd continued to be the top comedian on the Rolin lot. In 1918, he dropped Lonesome Luke and spent all of his time developing the new characterization in a long series of single reels. These were released for twenty-one months, until September, 1919, when *Bumping into Broadway*, the first double-reel comedy with the new Lloyd character, was put onto the market. Pathé had contracted with Roach in April for a series of nine Lloyd films.

This contract marked a turning point for Lloyd, both in his films and in his personal life. Bebe Daniels left Roach to join DeMille when her contract expired. He had offered her work the previous year, but Miss Daniels did not wish to jump her contract, preferring instead to work it out. Her last Lloyd film was the second of the new group, *Captain Kidd's Kids* (October, 1919). Roach and Lloyd decided that the new leading lady should be completely different from Bebe, and the blond actress acquired was Mildred Davis, whom Lloyd would later marry. She made her debut in the third two-reeler, *From Hand to Mouth* (November, 1919) and proved to be more than satisfactory. After *His Royal Slyness* (December, 1919), "Snub" Pollard moved over into his own series.

The first of the new series of Lloyd two-reelers had been completed by August, 1919, and Lloyd was asked to pose for publicity stills for use by Pathé in the distribution of his films. Arrangements were made to photograph these on Sunday, the twenty-fourth of August. The props for the picture-taking session were hurriedly assembled and inadvertently included among them was an overcharged papier-mâché bomb. As the shooting session progressed, the bomb was lighted and handed to Lloyd, who pressed it to his face and struck a funny pose. To Lloyd's great fortune, the photographer stopped to change his film holders, and Harold lowered the prop from his face. As he did, the bomb went off with terrific force.

The explosion cracked the ceiling, smashed windows, and split a pair of artificial teeth in the mouth of a bystander. Racked with pain, Lloyd was rushed to the hospital. He had lost the thumb and forefinger of his right hand and his face was badly burned. Doctors feared he would lose his sight completely as a result of the accident, and Lloyd was frightened lest they be correct.

This was a difficult time for the young comedian, whose career had really just begun to move. His will to regain his career remained strong throughout the next six months and, luckily, his sight was not affected. His face healed without leaving scars, and in March, 1920, he began work once again.

While he had been in the hospital, the last four films had been playing to large audiences. Even though Lloyd was inactive his popularity was mounting, and other companies began to approach him with contracts, hoping to lure him from Roach. Hal had made a smart business move as well as demonstrating his friendship when he increased Lloyd's percentage for the two-reel series. This move netted Harold over $100,000 on the films in distribution while he was incapacitated and guaranteed his future. Roach offered him a fifty-fifty partnership, but the comedian turned him down, not wishing to become involved with business problems.

Number Please, his last release of 1920, terminated the first Pathé contract, and Lloyd set about working on another group. Pathé had drawn up another new contract, which called for an additional six comedies over the next three years. These became Lloyd's bridge to features, for only one of the films contracted for was a double reel. The others were to be three or more reels in length. After finishing the fifth comedy, *A Sailor-Made Man*, Harold left short subjects for good.

The development of his comedy style in this second group of films is interesting. He began with *Now or Never* in three reels, the story of a reluctant baby sitter. His third, *I Do*, was done in three reels, but it did not go over with the preview audience. Then the suggestion was made that the first reel be eliminated because it did not move rapidly enough. This was done and the remaining footage became a hit, one which Lloyd was later to name as his best two-reel film. It was followed by *Never Weaken*, which was a refinement of the wild building-climbing episode Lloyd had first used in his 1918 *Look Out Below* (Many of Lloyd's films used the gimmick which required him to try to climb the side of a tall building. He used it again in the 1920 *High and Dizzy*.) *A Sailor-Made Man*, his fifth film in the series, was released in four reels. Both Roach and Lloyd wondered at its reception, but critics and audiences alike paid it tribute. Harold then went to work on the five-reel *Grandma's Boy*.

Pathé, extremely pleased with the results, wrote a new contract calling for another half-dozen Lloyd films, this time in five or more reels each. This was the ambition which Harold had been waiting to fulfill. Feature comedy could not succeed on gags alone—the comic had to be able to act. Lloyd's brand of comedy came naturally and easily to him. He was the best of the comics who were not really funny in themselves. Whereas, Keaton, Chaplin, or Langdon could have put poor material across by virtue of their pantomime, Lloyd relied almost entirely on his material. Given the same thing to work with, other comedians might have done as well. He did his tricks and gags with assurance but without bravado. Concerned with the writing of his pictures, Harold was dependably original, which was perhaps his most outstanding quality. His pictures had well-constructed plots and a tempo which increased in pace, reel by reel. His talent lay in the creation of fantastic and wholesome slapstick comedy.

Lloyd made nine more features in the silent era, of which *Safety Last* (1923) is the most famous. It was the story of a young country boy, clerking in a big city department store, who was forced to replace a professional climber and ascend the outside of the store wall as a publicity stunt. The climbing sequence occupied nearly three reels—half of the film—and it is still considered one of the greatest comedy stunts in film history. Although he worked above a wooden platform and made use of camera angles and careful editing, the climb is still realistic and impressive. (Remember, too, that Lloyd had only one good hand.)

The Freshman (1925) is another excellent and well-remembered feature comedy. Lloyd played a college student who dreamed of being the most popular boy on campus, even to the point of consenting to become a live tackle dummy for the football team. He eventually realized his dream by winning the big football game. The comedy highlight of this film came at a college dance which Harold attended in a tuxedo that was only temporarily sewed together. As the evening progressed the basting fell out and the suit unraveled, much to his chagrin. This comedy became Lloyd's greatest box-office success. With the succession of comedy hits behind him, it is little wonder that he had accumulated more than $15,000,000 by the end of the silent period.

Late in 1921, two other comedians joined the Rolin Company. Paul Parrott was given his own series, and his brother, Charles Parrott was put to work as writer, director, and occasional actor. Paul soon dropped his screen alias and went behind the camera to become better known under his own name (James Parrott) as the director of the Laurel and Hardy comedy shorts. Charles Parrott was popular with screen fans as Charlie Chase, and he soon began turning out a huge quantity of one- and two-reel films for Roach. Born in Baltimore in 1893, he had started in musical comedy and vaudeville before becoming a film comedian. His screen work with Keystone and other companies in the 1914–20 period had not been outstanding. On the other hand, Chase was a gifted director, and in this capacity he made many fine films with "Snub" Pollard and others on the Roach lot.

A tall, thin, dapper-looking fellow with a pencil moustache, Charlie Chase often played the serious young man whose sense of humor kept getting him into trouble. He was usually seen as the clumsy son who invariably upset mother or sweetheart, as the eager young fellow trying to get ahead, or as the husband who loved his wife but constantly found himself in marital hot water. His screen appearances became more interesting in the late twenties, when he abandoned slapstick and dealt with simple themes, as in *Movie Night* (May, 1929). This remains one of Charlie's best.

In this hilarious comedy, Charlie played the head of a household which went to the movies every Monday night for the weekly drawings held at the theater. The comedy began with Charlie's attempt to get his son (Spec O'Donnell) in for half-fare, continued through a riotous hiccup sequence with his little daughter (Edith Fellows), and ended in bedlam with his winning a live goose which got away.

A breezy sort of screen personality whose quizzical and disgusted looks were his biggest assets, Chase never achieved the fame he deserved in the silents. His versatility (he had made a good living singing, dancing, and playing various instruments) had to wait for sound before being rewarded. In the thirties, he made countless short subjects that were considerably better than his silents. Sound was the dimension which brought his screen appeal to its peak.

Hal Roach was trying hard to equal Sennett in the twenties, but his challenge never became a serious threat to the acknowledged master. He was unable to locate or develop another comic with the talent and appeal of Harold Lloyd. Roach signed Jimmy Finlayson, a noted Scottish comedian. But for one of those odd quirks in life, Finlayson would not have become a comic. He had been sent to college at Edinburgh by his well-to-do parents to study for a profession. While at Edinburgh, he became friendly with John Clyde, the famed Scottish actor and developed an intense interest in the stage. After playing both comedy and character roles in *Rob Roy*, he was offered a part in Graham Moffat's *Bunty Pulls the Strings* and toured the United States with the play. Jimmy reached Los Angeles in 1916 and decided to stay. After a brief stint with Thomas Ince and L-KO, he became a featured player in Sennett's Paramount comedies for more than a year before finally settling down with Roach. Off and on through the twenties, the small balding Scotsman was starred in different series, but could never quite make the grade at the box office. His greatest fame was yet to come in his supporting roles with Laurel and Hardy.

Will Rogers joined Roach in June, 1923, to make a series of twelve two-reelers. Very popular on the stage, Rogers had made a series of pictures for Samuel Goldwyn earlier, none of which were more than moderately successful. The silent medium was not suitable for his talents, but Will tried his best under Roach's direction.

The best of the lot was *Two Wagons, Both Covered* (January, 1924), a satire on the western epic which James Cruze had turned in under the Paramount banner. Will played a dual role, as trail scout and fancy dandy. He was definitely better in the former role as he lay across his horse and spat tobacco juice far and wide. Most of the humor, however, came from the subtitles. The surprise ending may have been a disappointment to some viewers. The audience had been primed to expect an Indian attack, and the Escrow Indians, as the title named them, turned out to be real estate agents waiting for new arrivals to California. But considering the land boom in the twenties, this gave a timely twist to the comedy.

Glen Tyron, Edgar Kennedy, Earl Mohan, Billy Engle, and Clyde Cook were also brought under the Roach banner with a reasonable degree of success, but no major personality appeared who could help Roach climb to Sennett's level. His greatest success at the time seemed to be in the children's comedies which he produced. Ernie Morrison, a small Negro boy billed as Sunshine Sammy, had supported first Lloyd and then Pollard before being starred in his own films. These were well received, and Roach conceived the idea of a comedy series using a group of juvenile actors. "Our Gang" comedies began with *One Terrible Day* (September, 1922) and continued as an unbroken series well into the thirties.

Featured in the original group were Mickey Daniels, Jackie Condon, Peggy Cartwright, and Ernie "Sunshine Sammy" Morrison. As the years went by, these child actors were joined by "Fat" Joe Cobb, Mary Kornman (the daughter of Lloyd's still photographer), Jackie Davis (the young brother of Lloyd's leading lady), Farina (played by Allan Hoskins), and Pete, the inevitable canine. The "Our Gang" series was very popular with audiences, and the young troupe took to the boards each year during the studio's month-long vacation to make personal appearances, which helped boost their appeal.

Roach, who never knew when something novel might turn into a hit, even cast a group of monkeys in the roles of humans and called the 1924 series *The Dippy Doo-Dads*.

After more than one hundred one-reel comedies, Harry "Snub" Pollard had been elevated to "full stardom" in 1922 with a series of double-reelers. Some of his finest work was done in these films, many of which were directed by Charles Parrott. *The Courtship of Miles Sandwich* (June, 1923) was an exceedingly funny burlesque of the traditional Thanksgiving story. After trying unsuccessfully to carve a turkey which was apparently made of cast iron, Snub finally succumbed to his boy's pleading question, "Why Thanksgiving?" Snub's version of the story was a unique combination of period dress and modern gadgets. In the Thanksgiving sequence, the Pilgrims drove Fords, rode horses, and passed the time skiing and smoking cigarets. Audiences roared.

Pollard's previous single-reel comedies had been little more than silly slapstick. They were often used by theaters as program fillers. *The Dumb Bell* (July, 1922) opened with Snub as an old man attended by six doctors who would not allow him to eat anything good. But Snub had hidden doughnuts on the drape rods which hung in the doorway between the rooms, and other unusual places were revealed as hiding places for food. Suddenly, the perspective changed, and Snub and the doctors were shown to be actors filming a movie before an ill-humored director. The owners of the studio promised Snub that he could have the director's job provided he could get rid of the temperamental artist. This was accomplished by some clever maneuvering, and Snub became the director. But in his new job Snub turned out to be even more temperamental than the ousted director, and the film ended with Snub smashing the set in an angry tantrum. This comedy short was weird, unrealistic, and actually not very funny, but its screwball humor was typical of the times.

Snub reached his stride in the two-reel shorts. He possessed the gift of imagination and had a keen sense of humor, but he had been limited by the hurried productions of the past. Now he had time to think and experiment. Without the bag of tricks that other comics had, Snub had to depend mainly upon characterization, a difficult feat in a single reel. It could be better accomplished in two thousand feet. With his roly-poly eyes, his quick, nervous manner, and his ever present drooping moustache, he soon developed the wacky form of slapstick for which he was best suited.

By the mid-twenties, Roach's film factory was producing a huge quantity of comedy shorts. Some of them were good to excellent, and some were very bad, but the majority were average, neither better nor worse than those produced by Rolin's competition. F. Richard Jones, who had directed for Sennett, supervised the production. There were many talented comics on the lot, but no real stars. It all amounted to a large and rather good comedy stock company made up of effective and devoted comedians under the direction of Robert McGowan, Charles Parrott, Stan Laurel, Ralph Cedar, George Jeske, and Percy Pembroke.

Always with an eye toward the unusual, Roach hit upon the idea of hiring former stars and building All-Star Comedies around them. Looking back now, it would appear that this was an act of desperation, but he apparently believed that Theda Bara, Harry Myers, Mabel Normand, and Agnes Ayres, among others, could be made profitable once again.

Stan Laurel had been on and off the Roach lot with some

regularity since his first appearance. Off the lot, he had made a series of six two-reelers for G. M. Anderson which were sold to Metro for release,[1] and another twelve for Standard Cinema which went to the screen bearing the Selznick label.[2] Between these two series, Laurel had done a great deal of writing and directing for Roach. Leo McCarey, who was to supervise the silent shorts of Laurel and Hardy, has credited Stan with a creative comic mind surpassed only by Chaplin.

It was late in December, 1926, during the production of one of the All Star Comedies, *Slipping Wives* (April, 1927), that Laurel returned to acting for good. This comedy starred Priscilla Dean and Herbert Rawlinson and called for two supporting roles —a lover and a butler. For the first time, Stan Laurel and Oliver Hardy appeared together in a Roach film.[3]

When the first All Star series ended, Roach began another series, the Hal Roach Comedy All Stars, as a substitute for the genuine star which he still lacked. Laurel and Hardy were an integral part of this new series, but they were still not playing leads together, although they appeared in several films which have since been called Laurel and Hardy comedies. For example, even though the two appeared in *With Love and Hisses* (August,

[1] Of these, *Mud and Sand* (November, 1922) is best remembered as the excellent comic take-off on the popular Rudolph Valentino and his recent hit, *Blood and Sand.*

[2] These two reelers were known in the trade as the Stan Laurel Comedies and were filmed at Universal, where the magnificent standing sets used in the current Universal features were utilized.

[3] These two had appeared together in a 1918 film entitled *Lucky Dog.* It had long been thought that this film had been lost forever, but a copy was turned up and used by Robert Youngson in one of his silent comedy compilations for 20th Century Fox. In one sequence, Hardy portrayed a robber who tried to relieve Stan of his money. Considering the fact that it would be almost ten years later when they began working as a team, some of the mannerisms which appear in *Lucky Dog* are amazing.

1927), Laurel and Jimmy Finlayson shared the billing in this comedy about army life.

It was not until Roach changed his distribution from Pathé to Metro-Goldwyn-Mayer that the Laurel and Hardy comedies came into existence. *Putting Pants on Philip* (December, 1927) was the first comedy made, but it was held back from release and was preceded by several others, including one of their most famous silent appearances, *The Second Hundred Years* (October, 1927). The trade papers immediately agreed that Roach had something in this team, and the boys were on their way. Hit after hit rolled out of the lot in rapid succession.[4]

The next year saw the pace continue with such classics as *Double Whoopee, Big Business,* and *Habeas Corpus.* The last film has been generally overlooked in favor of the more subtle comedies made by the team, but it ranks with their best in laugh-provoking situations. It opened with a mad doctor who needed a body for his experiments. His advertisement was answered by Stan and Oliver, and he offered them $500 to dig up a corpse for him. They agreed and left, but in the meantime, the doctor's butler, a secret agent, informed the police. The police picked up the lunatic, and the agent headed for the cemetery to apprehend the boys.

The scene changed to a dimly lighted road with Laurel and Hardy on their way. As could be expected, Oliver carried the lantern while Stanley struggled along with the heavy tools. Coming to an intersection, they argued which way to go. Stanley volunteered to climb what appeared to be a signpost to read the road directions, but Oliver decided to go up himself. After

[4] Every Laurel and Hardy fan remembers the fabulous pie-throwing in *The Battle of the Century* (December, 1927), the demolished house in *The Finishing Touch* (February, 1928), and the destruction of a string of autos from *Two Tars* (November, 1928).

139

much struggling, he finally made it to the top only to discover that the sign read WET PAINT. Climbing back down, the disgusted Oliver continued on his way, with Stanley and the tools close behind. At their destination, Oliver elected to stand guard while Stanley located the body and dug it up.

The agent was hidden inside the cemetery, but in a humorous turn of events he was accidentally knocked unconscious. When Stan came along, he put what he thought to be a body into his sack. On the way back, Oliver walked ahead with the lantern while Stanley trudged behind with the sack. Before long, a pair of feet poked through the sack and began walking, lessening the load for the weary Stan. The comedy ended in a denouement commonly used by the pair, with all three men stranded in one of those unbelievably deep puddles at a curb. The lively paced *Habeas Corpus* was not as restrained as much of their previous work. The absence of many of the pair's famous mannerisms in this film may be why film historians neglected it in favor of other, more typical comedies.[5]

Buster Keaton was introduced to the world of motion pictures during 1917 by Roscoe Arbuckle at the outset of his series for Joseph Schenck. Keaton, a well-known vaudeville trouper, had been in the entertainment business almost from birth. The son of Joseph H. Keaton, young Buster became a member of his father's act at the age of three months. The Three Keatons, as the act was then billed, featured acrobatics, and the boy appeared to be nearly indestructible as he was pushed, shoved, and thrown around the stage.

His interest in movies quickened when Arbuckle invited him to the studio to "see how it was done," and offered him a bit part in *The Butcher Boy* (April, 1917). Buster's scene with a quarter

---

[5] The only history of Laurel and Hardy is by John McCabe, *Mr. Laurel and Mr. Hardy*. The book is readable, but dates should be watched.

and molasses was an instant hit, and he turned down a much more lucrative stage offer to accept a contract at $200 a week to support Arbuckle. He appeared in twelve of the series and then enlisted in the U.S. Army in 1918, where he became a corporal while serving in France.

Returning from military service in 1919, Keaton made three more pictures with Arbuckle. When Arbuckle turned to feature comedy, Buster was offered a contract with Schenck to produce and star in his own series of two-reelers for Metro release. Keaton was given the Arbuckle unit (the Comique Film Corporation), and Schenck bought the old Chaplin lot in Hollywood for the first Keaton studio. Before starting work on his short subjects, Buster co-starred with William H. Crane in *The Saphead* (October, 1920), a five-reel film version of *The Henrietta,* for Metro release. His role was that of Bertie Van Alstyne, wealthy playboy, and he received raves from reviewers.

The first of his two-reel Metro comedies was *One Week* (September, 1920). Written and directed by Keaton and Eddie Cline, it co-starred Buster and Sybil Seely in a slapstick comedy of newlyweds who attempted to assemble a portable house. The numbers on the parts were mixed up, causing the walls to fall in and out. Other troubles were encountered, such as parts of the floor and ceiling falling, before a train came along and completely demolished the entire structure. This film was well received and was followed in October by *Convict 13.* Keaton portrayed an enthusiastic but inexperienced golfer who knocked himself senseless and dreamed that an escaped convict had traded clothes with him. In his dream, he was taken back to prison, and the fun began. Reviewers writing in the trade papers hailed this second comedy and placed Keaton in the front rank of screen comedians, even at this early stage in his career.

Scarecrow (November, 1920) left audiences and critics laughing long after the lights came back on. Keaton and Cline continued their madcap efforts with a slender plot (they were rivals for Sybil Seely) that ended with a chase on motorcycles. Buster won the chase and the girl. His last comedy of 1920, *Neighbors* (December), also had little plot, but Buster made the most of it. The action took place in two tenement houses with a fence between them. Buster wanted to marry Virginia Fox, his pretty neighbor on the other side of the fence, but neither his parents nor hers would give their consent, and so he planned a three-story elopement. Keaton's amazing acrobatic ability was put to good use in this story. His stunts on the fence, its gate, the clothes line, and the telephone poles inside the yard were daring and breath-taking. As with his previous releases, this one was greeted with much enthusiasm.

In 1921, Keaton made four additional two-reelers for Metro before Schenck moved to Associated First National for release. For this company Keaton produced eleven double-reel comedies, and it was in this group that his best short comedy was conceived. *Cops* (March, 1922) easily ranks as one of the finest pieces of comic action ever put before the camera. Written and directed by Keaton and Cline, the film opened with Buster having problems with his girl (Virginia Fox). She would not marry him until he had made a success of himself. Buster, sitting dejected and stone-faced on a curb, told his troubles to a man who proceeded to swindle him out of his savings by selling him a dilapidated horse and wagon. The broken-down nag looked as if it could never move, but Buster treated the horse as if it were Man o' War.

As Buster drove proudly down the street, he was stopped by a man who mistook him for a furniture mover. This was his first chance to earn some money, so Buster helped the man load

Ford Sterling was the Chief of the Keystone Cops and Sennett's most popular comic until Chaplin came along.

Courtesy Don Overton

Charlie's brother-in-law, played by Bull Montana, was not one to tangle with. The former athlete was in great demand in pictures of the twenties. (Note the spelling "Charley" in the upper lefthand corner. "Charlie" was more commonly used, however. This is an example of the charming but sometimes confusing inconsistencies of the silent period.)

Courtesy Don Overton

Charlie Chase gets some needed cleaning up in this scene from
Dog Shy (1926).

Courtesy Don Overton

Madeline Hurlock and a curious Billy Bevan brought zest and laughs to *From Rags to Britches*, a 1925 comedy for Mack Sennett.

Courtesy Don Overton

WILLIAM FOX PRESENTS
AL ST. JOHN
IN
"SPECIAL DELIVERY"

Al St. John demonstrates one of the tricks he learned at Keystone
in this scene from a two-reel Fox comedy of 1922,
Special Delivery.

Courtesy Sam Grossman

Buster Keaton can't quite understand the large police escort for
his wagonload of furniture in *Cops* (1922).

Courtesy Nick Fiorentino

Sad-faced Harry Langdon was one of the great clowns of silent comedy.

Courtesy of Larry Edmunds Bookshop

Time has mistreated the comic on the left. His name has been forgotten, but *Our Gang* fans will remember Sunshine Sammy and little Mary Kornman.

Courtesy Fred Newmeyer

the furniture on the wagon, took the address, and started across town to deliver his load. On the way, he inadvertently got in the middle of the annual police parade. A modest hero, he waved to the cheering crowd.

Suddenly an anarchist lighted a bomb and threw it from a rooftop into the midst of the parade. The bomb landed conveniently on the wagon beside Buster, who was looking for a match. He lit his cigaret and casually tossed the bomb over his shoulder. The explosion caused a riot in the crowd, the parade, and the reviewing stand, where his sweetheart happened to be sitting. Obviously, this was Buster's cue to make a hasty exit, which he did, and the chase was on. In the process, the wagon and all of the furniture were destroyed. Buster, on foot and followed by what appeared to be a regiment of angry police, went up and down streets, through alleys, and around corners. Many fine bits of comedy action occurred as the chase increased frantically, finally culminating with the entire police force behind lock and key as Keaton emerged the lone victor. But when he was once again rejected by his humiliated sweetheart, Buster returned to the jail, unlocked the door, and was summarily hauled inside as the reel faded.

Twelve feature-length comedies for Schenck followed the series of two-reelers. Nine of these were released by Metro and its successor Metro-Goldwyn-Mayer. The remaining three were distributed by United Artists. *Sherlock Jr.* (April, 1924) was his shortest feature, consisting of five reels containing 4,065 feet. It was also one of his cleverest comedies. The simple plot, a satire on the typical movie mystery, served only as a framework for the gags. Buster portrayed a day-dreaming movie projectionist. The sequence in which he walked on the beam of light from the projection booth to the stage received many accolades, as did the segment which found Buster shooting a game of pool with the villain (Ward Crane), blissfully unaware that one of the balls was actually a concealed bomb.

Keaton's comic genius reached its peak in *The General*, an eight-reel United Artists release of 1927, which many critics declare to be the last great comedy of the silent screen. Taking a footnote from history, *The General* was loosely built around the story of the Andrews raid. James J. Andrews (the Northern spy who stole a train from the South during the Civil War) was mostly ignored in Keaton's film, and the story revolved around Johnnie Gray and his pet, a big black locomotive named "The General." In love with Annabelle Lee (Marion Mack), Johnnie was determined to prove himself, and what better way was there than to enlist in the army? Unfortunately, even the Southern army didn't want him. Meanwhile, his beloved engine had been stolen. While trying to regain it, he stumbled onto a Northern staff conference and discovered that Annabelle was being held captive. After various trials, tribulations and bits of side-splitting comedy, "The General" was regained, an army commission was forthcoming, and Keaton was safe in Annabelle's arms.

The General, taken as a whole, was more rapidly paced than most of Buster's comedies, even though it contained the longest chase sequence in comedy history, occupying seven of the eight reels. However, the gags were deliberately spaced throughout the strong story line, and the entire film became a wonderful example of Keaton's craftsmanship. Some critics have suggested the the film's construction was balanced and precise in its conception and execution. The balance was most certainly there, but its precision came from Keaton's long and rich experience in comedy. Most Keaton admirers will agree that he never made a poor comedy in the silent days.

Keaton's entire background, like Chaplin's, had been in the

field of comic entertainment, and he knew, almost as if he possessed a sixth sense, how and when to get a laugh. His art was essentially pantomimic, and as long as silent pictures reigned, Keaton's visual gags were greatly appreciated by audiences. His formula, like the formulas of Chaplin and Lloyd was simple—the small man against the big world. Keaton differed from them in that his portrayals were always of the eternal pessimist. Nor did Buster try to gain audience sympathy. His screen character believed that no matter how hard he tried, things would somehow go wrong, and after a time he just stopped trying and left things to Fate. The lucky break that occasionally came along simply served to remind him that harder times lay ahead. His heroines were generally dumber than he, if that was possible. Just as Keaton would get things straightened out and moving along satisfactorily, his girl would somehow undo all of his efforts in no time at all. He therefore usually managed to come out behind the eight-ball, as in *The Cameraman* (September, 1928). As a newsreel photographer hoping to get a scoop, he jumped on a fire engine as it roared by, only to find that it was *returning* from the fire.

Although Keaton had broken his leg in 1922 and his neck in 1924, he rarely used a double, and some of his stunts were truly fantastic. He dropped eighty-five feet from a suspension bridge into a net for *The Paleface* (January, 1922). In *Hard Luck* (March, 1921), he had to dive from a fifty-foot platform, miss a swimming pool, and crash through a marble pavement (paper covered with wax). Probably the most thrilling of all was his wild ride on the handlebars of a motorcycle for *Sherlock Jr.* Keaton always proved to the audience that what they saw was real, not a miracle provided by the camera or an editor, by performing his stunts in a long shot without a cut.

Many appraisals of Keaton's creative genius have been made.

145

Keaton was the equal of Chaplin in every respect, but he presented a picture of cold, unsentimental innocence as opposed to Chaplin's pathos. His films, made from bare outlines rather than detailed shooting scripts, have firmly established his place in the wonderful world of laughter. This place in the top ranks of screen comedians is based on a much smaller output than that of either Chaplin or Lloyd. Buster did not have to struggle for recognition like Lloyd, nor did his screen character go through a long evolutionary process as did Chaplin's. In terms of box-office receipts, he ranked behind both Chaplin and Lloyd, but smooth and polished, his work stands up better today than that of his contemporaries, whose pictures have become dated to a much greater extent.

The Chaplin of the twenties was a consummate artist, the one comic whose universality was recognized, acknowledged, and appreciated. His work had a lyrical quality about it that set him far above the average. Gone was the farce, the knock-about action, the crude slapstick. These elements of his early films had been replaced with qualities of the human character which drew sympathy from all audiences, regardless of age. His techniques had become fully developed, and his mastery of them was evident, beginning with his contract at First National in 1918.

A Dog's Life (April, 1918) has been acclaimed by most critics for its realistic treatment of a strong story, filled with straight drama relieved by comic touches. Especially praised has been the sequence at the employment office where Charlie was shouldered from window to window, barely losing out on the available jobs until there were none left. The precision in this scene bordered on ballet. *Shoulder Arms* (October, 1918) mixed realism with fantasy and became Chaplin's masterpiece up to that time. Filled with satirical thrusts toward war, the story told of an average man who was inducted into the army and sent to France. Although the camouflage-tree scene is probably the best remembered, others, such as Charlie's tribulations in attempting to sleep in a water-filled dugout, deserve mention. The humor in Charlie's lifting his soaking pillow from the water, fluffing it up, and replacing it before he retired came not so much from what was done as how it was accomplished. Chaplin's matchless touch was unmistakably there.

Sunnyside (June, 1919) was a peculiar film, not quite a comedy or a drama, and does not represent the Chaplin with whom we are familiar. Meant to be satire, the three-reel story was logical and its production was polished, but it did not amuse audiences. The film's poetry and lyricism were all praised but comedy *is* comedy, and Chaplin was warned that his competitors were getting far more laughs. *A Day's Pleasure* (December, 1919) established a different mood from his three previous First National comedies, but it brought back the laughs. It was also unlike Chaplin's usual material in that the comedy device of repetition was much overworked, gag after gag being repeated almost to the point of boredom.

Chaplin was producing fewer films and taking more time with them. His productions were tasteful, but expensive. He thought nothing of shooting sixty to ninety thousand feet of film for a two-reel comedy, and he often exposed half a million feet for a feature. Charlie was fortunate that the popularity of his films around the world allowed such extravagance. His features took a year or more to make, and he had a habit of disappearing for indefinite periods of time to think out ideas or to brood over his personal life. Chester Conklin recalled one occasion when Chaplin was shooting *The Gold Rush* (August, 1925). In the middle of a conference, Charlie absent-mindedly inquired of a secretary when the next ship left for England. Shortly after receiving a reply, he disappeared and failed to show up for work for three months. After spending a few frantic days searching for him, his staff finally recalled the query. Checking with the steamship lines, they discovered what had happened. Chaplin paid each and every member of the crew and cast during such a break. His salary scale was not the highest in Hollywood, but as Chester put it, "Sign on with Charlie for a picture and you were sure of eating for a year or more."

One of Chaplin's best-known pictures and his first starring feature (discounting *Tillie's Punctured Romance,* which he neither produced nor starred in), *The Kid* (February, 1921) required more than a year to make and cost around $300,000. Charlie's First National contract called for a basic two reels and allowed $15,000 per reel above that. Knowing that such an arrangement would not cover the production costs for *The Kid* and feeling that it was worth more, Chaplin entered into negotiation with First National, which was reluctant to pay more. Chaplin's persistence won, however, and he received $600,000 plus 75 per cent of the $2,500,000 that it grossed.

So great was the financial and critical success which greeted *The Kid* that Chaplin's next two comedies came as something of a letdown. *The Idle Class* (September, 1921) was reminiscent of the Mutual shorts but had a slower tempo and fewer laughs. *Pay Day* (April, 1922) recalled the Chaplin of Essanay days. Its major achievement was its technical quality, with backlighting being used for the interior shots and some interesting night scenes.

The Pilgrim (February, 1923) was a welcome return to the characteristic Chaplin—the nose-thumber of convention—and completed his First National contract. As an escaped convict masquerading as a minister, Charlie had an opportunity to deliver a pantomime sermon on David and Goliath, the highlight of the film and the equal of any of his comic bits. After *The Kid,* Chaplin had made two more shorts, but from *The Pilgrim* on, all his films were features.

In the next eight years Chaplin was to make only three films in which he starred. His first two films for United Artists were the fulfillment of an earlier dream and a promise. Charlie had always wanted to make one big dramatic feature to prove that he was more than just a comedian. He had started a drama at Essanay (entitled *Life*), but it was never finished. He had also promised Edna Purviance that he would make her a dramatic actress and, to this end, Chaplin produced *A Woman of Paris* (October, 1923). The film, although a critical success, did not do well at the boxoffice and virtually ended Miss Purviance's career. The public would not accept her in the role of a worldly woman.

Of his last silent features, only *The Circus* (January, 1928) failed to score a hit. It contained nothing ingenious or new, as did his greatest successes, *The Gold Rush* and *City Lights* (February, 1931). The latter was two years in the making, used 800,000 feet of film, cost over one million and a half dollars, was released nearly three years after sound had become accepted as the norm, and still was a smashing success.

Chaplin had come a long way from the early Keystone days when the hesitant little Englishman first presented himself to Mack Sennett. He had become the acknowledged master of comedy, a man whose name was a household word. A simple picture or lantern slide of him was enough to tell people that his films were playing. He had made a fortune and had hobnobbed with the social lions of two continents. Charlie was completely independent, and it showed in his films. Many critics have attempted to explain his popularity,[6] but perhaps the simplest explanation

[6] For perhaps the best metaphysical and intellectual discussion, see Robert Payne, *The Great Charlie,* published in this country as *The Great God Pan.*

is his universal appeal and the greatness of his vigorous talent. He could be looked up to, laughed at, and pitied, almost at once. It was part of Chaplin's genius that he could make audiences become aware of and sympathetic to the human condition—they "laughed lest they cry."[7]

One of the most popular comedians of his day was Larry Semon, who for a time came close to Chaplin, Lloyd, and Keaton in popularity. However, he was not as ingenious or as inventive in his comic characterizations, and both he and his pictures have become obscure today. Few recall or mention his work with other than fleeting praise. Wearing a bowler hat and trousers with the waistline at his chest and invariably held up by suspenders, little white-faced Larry tumbled his way through more than sixty single- and double-reel comedies while with Vitagraph. He then went on to make a number of comedies for Chadwick, Educational, and Pathé.

The son of a professional magician (Zera the Great), Semon was born in West Point, Mississippi, on July 16, 1889. As a youth he possessed enough artistic talent to attend art school after graduation from a Savannah, Georgia, high school. This led to a position as cartoonist on the old *New York Sun*. His evenings were spent with amateur dramatics, which resulted in a job as director for Frank Daniels at Vitagraph. He soon began writing and starring in Vitagraph comedies himself, thus giving much-needed balance to the firm's program. Their leading comedy stars at that time were Hughie Mack, Earl Montgomery, and Joe Rock, all knockabout comics.

Larry was an agile acrobatic clown whose comedy may not have been strikingly original, and he was not enough of a comedian by himself to succeed without the aid of a gimmick, but he became extremely clever in the use of visual mechanical gags

[7] Cotes and Niklaus, *The Little Fellow*, New York, Citadel Press, 1965.

and he was a great exponent of the chase. In many ways he was similar to Harold Lloyd—it was his material that made him. Larry carried the key to his success as a comedian in the back pocket of his high pants. In a small, fat, black leather notebook, he kept a careful record of all his ideas, jokes, and variations on old visual themes. This notebook was worth many thousands of dollars to him and served more or less as the script for whatever comedy he was working on at the time.

Like the other top comics, Semon drove himself hard to perfect these sight gags. He had the knack of knowing a good joke when he saw it. He expected everyone who worked with him to take comedy as seriously as he did. He has been credited with saying, "A comedy is only as funny as its gags; the comic is secondary." By 1922, when he was earning $2,000 a week, he demanded that the thirty-two people in his unit eat, sleep, read, and think gags.

By contrast, in his films he accepted the perfectly ridiculous situations he encountered as if they were the most natural things in the world, questioning nothing but going on his merry way with the simple grin that became part of his trademark. He often portrayed the "dumb bell," the poor fool who avoided violence but who somehow always wound up in the middle of rough and tumble play. *Dunces and Danger* (August, 1918) was an early example of a formula from which Semon seldom varied. In this single reel, Larry and his wife were vaudeville actors down on their luck. While his wife washed the clothes, Larry cooked dinner—a chicken foot. A cracker broken in half served as an appetizer. The pantomime was rich and varied as both suddenly filled up to avoid eating the undesirable chicken foot. Patting themselves on the stomach in a self-satisfying way, both proclaimed that they couldn't eat another bite.

The tempo of this leisurely opening was suddenly disrupted

by a knock at the door. A peek outside the door soon let the audience in on the fun ahead—bill collectors! Of course, Semon was completely broke, so the collectors took his trunks, washing, and whatever else they could get their hands on. Refusing to admit the others who rapidly fell into line outside their door, Larry and wife prepared to exit through the window to the roof. Their adversaries peeked through the keyhole in time to view the preparations for escape, and a race for the roof began between the protagonists and their opponents. There was some tricky acrobatic maneuvering on the rooftops before the two climbed down the side of the building on a teetering ladder, only to fall back through their own window at the feet of the fast-moving bill collectors. Fortunately, one of the men turned out to be a lawyer with a million-dollar bequest for the hapless couple, bringing the action to a happy, if improbable close.

Bathing Beauties and Big Boobs (July, 1918) contained gags which Semon used many times with some variation. This time, Larry had trouble with his girl's father at the beach. Father did not think Larry worthy of his daughter, so Semon and a friend decided to fake a robbery and set Larry up as the hero. While Larry was passing the loot to his friend outside, real thugs made off with it. The chase was on, with Larry after the crooks and Father after Larry. It shifted from land to speedboats on the water, and at one point, after Semon had recovered the money and was in the process of escaping from the thieves, he swung out over the ocean on a rope, only to have it break as he reached the apex of its swing, dumping him into the ocean. A fine variation of this incident was used years later in *The Sawmill* (January, 1922).

Six weeks were spent making *The Grocery Clerk* (January, 1920), Semon's first release that year. In general, it was a continuation of the same type of material he had been using for years, but it was a winning formula and Larry saw no reason to change it. Semon played something of a supporting role in the film, for the hit of *The Grocery Clerk* was an actor who worked without pay—a fuzzy-haired cat.

The Sportsman (January, 1921) portrayed Semon in a mythical kingdom where he was always being chased about by several strange individuals. It became apparent that the chase was simply contrived to provide an excuse for the slapstick. When Semon wasn't tumbling into water, falling through trapdoors, crawling under rugs, or being speared from behind, the camera was trying to camouflage the film's lack of coherence by resorting to various photographic tricks.

One of the most imaginative and interesting films Semon ever made was *The Sawmill*. Larry played the bungling simpleton in a lumber camp. He spent most of his time trying to keep out of trouble and out of the clutches of his foreman (Oliver Hardy). When the owner came to visit his property, he became the brunt of a number of accidents in which he was struck on the head, knocked over, and covered with paint. The foreman was fired for incompetence(because of Semon, naturally), and Larry became the hero of the day by saving the owner's daughter (Dorothy Dwan) and his money from the disgusted Hardy, who was seeking revenge. One of the best scenes in this two-reeler had Semon smoking his pipe while sitting on a log, blissfully unaware that the log was moving towards a huge sawblade. The saw missed Larry, but his trousers were snagged and ripped off. Attempting to change clothes, Larry was forced to run from cabin to cabin as falling trees destroyed them one by one.

The Sawmill marked the deterioration of a relationship between Semon and Vitagraph that had been stormy almost from the beginning. Larry spent much of his free time worrying about everything—his films, his popularity, production costs, and the future. An affable fellow off the set, he had the temperament of a prima donna when working. He despised working with anyone who could or might steal the limelight from him. When a day's rushes proved to benefit others more than himself, he was not above rewriting the story to reduce the role of those who stole the scene. As Semon became better known, he began to be increasingly suspicious of his colleagues and worriedly devoted more and more time to success. These worries about his work and his future finally led to disagreements with Albert E. Smith, the head of Vitagraph. The company financed and distributed Semon's comedies, which were tremendous money-makers. Larry directed or co-directed his own pictures, and the production status of his films had generally been left to his judgment.

Larry was refused a higher budget which he felt would improve his work. However, his renewal contract called for fewer pictures, which gave him more time to plan the execution of his comedy ideas. In some ways this was equivalent to a higher budget, but Larry was still unsatisfied. As he devoted even more time to his comedies and exceeded his budgetary limits, Vitagraph's profits began to diminish. Semon was lavish with production money. He had spent nearly three months on location making *The Sawmill*. Concerned with the comfort of his crew, Larry had had permanent log cabins and buildings constructed on the location site to house the entire crew with all the comforts of home. This was too much for Smith, who insisted that Semon become his own producer. The company would continue to release his films, but it would not agree to foot the bills which he claimed were necessary. A long period of bickering followed until Vitagraph finally refused to renew his contract, and Semon set out on his own.

Larry made a six-reel feature, *The Girl in the Limousine*, for First National in 1924, and then did a series of two-reel shorts along with some feature work for Chadwick, which released through Educational. During this time he also produced features for Pathé release and directed Alice Day for Sennett. These films received adverse criticism, and receipts fell at the box office. His October, 1927, release, *The Stuntman,* was panned by *Film Daily's* short-subject section in its October 2 issue: "Semon wrote and directed this himself, which may be what's wrong with it. As a black face comedian [Semon played in black face for this one film. His usual make-up was a very white face with emphasized black eyes, eyebrows, and lips.], he is in the average run of that type, but he should let someone specializing in that work write his gags. . . . [He] will have to do better than this if he wants to get the real money."

His film *Dummies* (January, 1928) was just a rehash of worn-out jokes. Semon's time was over. At one time worth a quarter of million dollars, he declared personal bankruptcy on March 19, 1928, listing liabilities of $454,639 and assets of $300. He left pictures and went to work in a New York vaudeville circuit. The high-strung little clown soon after suffered a nervous breakdown complicated by pneumonia. Death came to the youthful comedian on October 8, 1928. Discouraged, destitute, and *persona non grata* in filmland, Semon worried himself to death, in the opinion of his friends and co-workers.

Looking back upon his career and the films that he made, it it not too difficult to understand Semon's popularity. On-screen he was often a fascinating clown. Although creative in the use of his gags, he repeated his successful routines until they were tiresome clichés. Many of his comedies satirized human follies. His failure to rank as a top comedian seems to have derived from the same difficulty in bridging the gap between success and greatness that circumscribed Lupino Lane's career. Neither Semon nor Lane had the "extra something" to sustain their careers. In

Semon's case, part of the blame lay with the comic personality and his material. Semon was like Harold Lloyd in many ways, but Lloyd had the material *and* the personality that gave his comedies an emotional depth lacking in Semon's. Semon's films contained no rhythmical construction; very often they were but a series of gags loosely strung together, uneven and without unity. Little time was wasted establishing a thin plot line, and the rest of the film was devoted to one or more chases. In these chases Semon often excelled, and at their best they were wild, fast, and funny. They formed part of the basis and conviction of Semon's screen comedy. Had he been more of a personality, it is possible he could have created an image as enduring as the images of the comedians he challenged briefly in his prime.

CHAPTER TEN

One Led, Others Followed

THE Sennett of the twenties was not the Sennett of Keystone or Triangle. Times had changed. Audience taste in comedy had become more sophisticated. No one was more aware of this change in public taste than Mack Sennett, and that fact helps to explain his long period of prosperity and popularity in the world of motion pictures. His closest competitors, Hal Roach and Al Christie, could do little more than challenge his position as the undisputed King of Comedy.

Sennett's films for Paramount showed the beginning of a modification in his style. The days of wild slapstick were over.

He relied on fast-moving backgrounds, slow-moving mechanical gags, and camera tricks to create laughter in the twenties. The circular panorama on the Sennett lot provided the necessary background for a speedy, effective, but inexpensive and easily arranged chase. While the background revolved in one direction, a treadmill with the comedian operated in the opposite direction.

When viewed today, the mechanical gags become almost unbearable. At the sight of a pretty girl, a man's moustache would curl and uncurl several times in slow motion. When he was kissed, the toes of his shoes might also curl in the same manner. Approaching danger would be the cue for curly hair to straighten and straight hair to curl. Repetition of such gags, combined with scenes that were too long or subtitles that strained for humor, detracted from otherwise excellent comedies. Occasionally, touches of the old Sennett would emerge to be savored. As the passing years demanded more and more of his time for business matters, it is understandable that his comedies just prior to the sound era in some ways lacked the inventiveness of the fabled Keystones. For the most part, the madness and mayhem evident in his earlier comedies no longer existed.

Production had become highly systematized, but the master made fewer films than any of his competition. He moved into the area of feature comedy with *Down on the Farm* (April, 1920), *Married Life* (June, 1920), and *A Small Town Idol* (February, 1921). These films were successful financially but not to the degree necessary to allow him to stop making the short subjects. Sennett was clever enough to realize that his future was still in the short comedy field, and it remained his area of concentration, with an occasional feature thrown in for good measure.

Mack Sennett was fortunate in several ways. Although his stars and directors came and left, he had the ability to hire and maintain what amounted to the best group of comedy favorites

Larry Semon is about to leave home in this scene from *Dummies* (1928), a double-reel Chadwick production, released through Educational.

Courtesy Don Overton

The struggling author –
not much of an author –
but a good struggler.

Jimmy Finlayson wonders about Theda Bara's intentions in *Madame Mystery* (1926). The picture was one of Hal Roach's attempts to resurrect the value of former box-office greats.

Courtesy Don Overton

There is no need to ask Andy Clyde "Who's in charge here?" in this scene from *Taxi Beauties,* one of the films in the "Taxi Driver" series released in 1928–29.

This "building-climbing" sequence from *Never Weaken* (1921)
became typical in some of Harold Lloyd's comedies.

Courtesy Don Overton

Although this scene did not come from one of Harold Lloyd's
short comedies, it is typical of Lloyd's light treatment of a serious
situation. The picture was *Why Worry?* (1923).

Courtesy Fred Newmeyer

Natalie Kingston can't believe what she sees. Actually, it's a love-sick Ben Turpin in *The Daredevil*.

Romeo (Ben Turpin) takes leave of his fair Juliet (Madeline Hurlock) in the 1924 *Romeo and Juliet.*

Courtesy 8mm Collector

Ben Turpin strikes a western pose for Phyllis Haver during the
filming of *A Small Town Idol* (1921).

under one studio roof. With the exception of Chaplin, no comedian who left Sennett ever attained greater fame than he had while with him. He retained his deft touch for selecting funny subject matter, and several of the gems of silent screen parody came from this time. Toward the end of the twenties, he brought out many comedies starring Carole Lombard, Johnny Burke, and Eddie Quillan that were more sophisticated and had a more complicated plot than characterization—comparable to some of the situation comedies on television. These films no longer used a thread to hang the plots on, but were filled with characters and had many twists and turns in the story. The films were popular and in certain ways indicated the sort of comedy that sound would bring.

One of Sennett's most durable comedians to find favor at the box office was little Billy Bevan, an Australian who first played minor supporting roles in the Paramount comedies. Billy's film career dated back to 1917 when he supported Neal Burns at L-KO, but it failed to get off the ground until he signed with Sennett. His rise began in earnest with *Let 'Er Go* (May, 1920), and Bevan was soon a stable fixture in the Sennett releases for Associated First National and then Pathé.

One of his early hits was *Ma and Pa* (June, 1922) with Mildred June. The film began with the wedding of Billy and Mildred. It then cut to five years later. Billy was washing his kids and hanging them out on the line to dry. He was now an accomplished paper hanger, but he had ambitions for the theatrical life. Billy got a good job papering the apartment of an actress who had promised him a part in her play. At her apartment Billy began work, but he was so elated at the prospect of finally becoming a part of the theater that he papered over all the doors and windows. Kicked out by the actress' husband, Bevan went over to the theater to claim his job. The remainder of the film

159

was devoted to inane mayhem as our hero managed to destroy the stage production before it even got under way.

Bevan was at home with some of the fantastic material that Sennett comedians had to work with during the twenties. *A Sea Dog's Tale* (July, 1926) took place in "Salami, a link of the Sausage Islands." Princess Vanilla (Madeline Hurlock) fell in love with Wilbur Watts (Bevan) from a picture of him in a newspaper. King Gumbo (Andy Clyde) offered a full pardon to Jo Jo (Vernon Dent), provided he could produce Billy. Jo Jo had been sentenced to death for accidentally pushing the King into a cauldron of boiling water, which had singed the royal dignity. A cutaway shot took the viewer to the United States, where poor Billy was being forced to marry his landlady (Patsy O'Byrne) in lieu of his back rent. Kidnapped by Jo Jo's men and taken to the island, he was greatly relieved by the King's proposition of marriage to Vanilla.

A banquet held in Billy's honor was pure farce. The native waiter served the soup with a sponge. One look at this strange custom and Billy decided he would forego the entree. Motioning his disapproval to the waiter, he watched in open-mouthed amazement as the waiter dipped the sponge back in his bowl, drained it dry, and squeezed the sponge out above the next guest's bowl. Served spaghetti, Billy stared at the others, who dipped into their plates for a handful, whirled it around, and stuffed the food into their mouths. He tried the same method but lost his spaghetti as it sailed across the table and into King Gumbo's face. As a fitting punishment for this grave offense, Jo Jo (who desired Vanilla for himself) suggested that Billy do battle with the sacred sharks.

Bevan was dumped into the ocean with great ceremony. Other Bevan comic highlights followed. He struck a match to see underneath the water. Throwing the match away, he set fire to the ocean floor, but finally extinguished the flames. Wearing a starfish for a badge, he directed traffic for the fish. He met a lovely mermaid while on duty and dallied for a while. Unknown to him, his frustrated bride-to-be was hovering above in an airplane. Suddenly, an anchor plunged into the water, caught his trousers, and hauled the bewildered Bevan up to the aircraft. When Billy discovered his rescuer to be his landlady, he jumped out, preferring to return to his new underwater friend.

Bevan was a comedian who worked for his laughs and worked hard. He was a dumpy little fellow full of self-assurance, his brush moustache being his greatest asset. With it, he could impersonate a Wall Street banker and look the part. Without it, he seemed almost a different person and was not nearly so humorous. The moustache added just the correct amount of dignity to Billy's bearing to make the comedy action that much more ridiculous and, in turn, funnier. It is worth noting that without his moustache, he was not as good a box-office draw.

He made a shambles of the national pastime with his curve ball in *Butter Fingers* (August, 1925). Even polo did not escape his practiced eye in *Giddap* (March, 1925). *A Small Town Princess* (March, 1927), *The Bull Fighter* (May, 1927), and *Flirty Four-Flushers* (December, 1926) were four examples of his comedy sans moustache. As Archibald de Shyster in the last-mentioned film, he set out to marry a wealthy girl. Madeline Hurlock, as Aggie, was a waitress who wanted to wed a rich man. When she won a vacation at a fashionable hotel in a contest, she decided that her chance had arrived. Vernon Dent played Brown, the genuine millionaire. The basic ingredients for fun were there, but somehow the comedy never quite came off.

Bevan was fortunate to have the assistance of such top supporting actors as Miss Hurlock, Vernon Dent, and Andy Clyde. Although Miss Hurlock was not really a comedienne, she was a beautiful addition to the scenery and handled her roles in a competent manner. Del Lord, Roy Del Ruth, Harry Edwards, and other first-rate comedy directors handed Billy in a way that kept him a top attraction in the Sennett ranks for a decade.

Of all the comedians on the Sennett lot in the twenties, none came closer to true artistry than a pathetically shy little clown named Harry Langdon. Born in Council Bluffs, Iowa, Harry had started life as a newsboy in the theatrical district of Omaha, Nebraska. In 1896, at the age of twelve, he began a career in vaudeville that took him through traveling medicine troupes, carnivals, circuses, and musical comedy until he eventually wound up with Sennett in late 1923.

Beginning with *Picking Peaches* (February, 1924), Langdon romped his way through twenty-three short comedies, each a step forward toward perfection of his screen character. In his films, the sad-faced Harry portrayed an innocent whose comic simplicity in a world he could not begin to comprehend always left him amazed at what transpired before him, but he usually came out on top without knowing exactly how. Blind faith in humanity carried him through all difficulties to the finish. A gesture that became his trademark symbolized it all. His odd, hesitant wave of the hand and his big eyes with their owlish blink of humility told the world that he was eager to be friends with it but was uncertain that he was good enough.

The fact that Langdon achieved such fame in a comparatively small number of shorts is an indication of his genius. Harry came close to true art, but, unfortunately, just as his screen character reached maturity, he decided to try feature comedies. Harry Edwards, and later Frank Capra, understood better than Harry himself the proper way to nurture and use his talents. When Langdon decided to write, direct, produce, and star in his own features, he created the situation that ultimately became his undoing. Even though his first two features rank among the best ever made, each feature was less successful than its predecessor, and Harry probably never really understood where he failed.

Langdon was not ready for feature work—not in the way he approached it. Pushing the plot to one side and neglecting comic invention, he appears to have concentrated on large doses of pathos and pantomime. His comedy style, which was still developing, did not have the needed variety for the use to which Harry put it. With the exception of Keaton, Harry was the only major comic who attempted to turn out two features a year. His brand of comedy, which required a sympathetic audience, failed to realize its promise, and the features ended his career. First National, which released them, did not renew its contract with Langdon in 1928, and although he sought release through United Artists, Harry was finished.

In many of his films, Harry was cast in ludicrous situations. As an ambitious but patient photographer, he matched wits with a demonic kid in *Smile Please* (March, 1924). *Feet of Mud* (December, 1924) found him a substitute football player who wanted to stay benched but had to play instead. Given a political job (street cleaner) by his girl's father, he inadvertently became involved with a secret Chinese society and managed to get mixed up in a tong war, but of course rescued his sweetheart at the end. He ducked shells as a soldier in *All Night Long* (November, 1924) and dodged falling trees as a lumberjack mistaken for a desperate criminal in *Boobs in the Woods* (February, 1925).

One of his unforgettable roles came with *His Marriage Wow* (March, 1925). The film opened at the church where Natalie Kingston anxiously awaited her groom. The camera then cut to poor Harry, sitting alone in the pew of another church, apparently at a loss to explain why no one else had showed up, but trying very hard to maintain his calm dignity without appearing overly concerned about the puzzling situation. When Harry paid for the ceremony in advance, a brief word with the minister finally brought the realization that he was in the wrong church. A feeble attempt to regain his money from the recalcitrant minister preceded his mad dash out of the church and down the street.

In the meantime, a certain pessimistic Professor McGlum was trying to console Natalie by telling her that Harry was probably dead. The audience knew better, as Harry came sailing down the street to an intersection where he thoroughly confused a policeman on duty by his request for directions. Receiving them, he shot off again but soon came racing down another street back to the same intersection. After another bout with the policeman and an episode with a man who wanted a match, Harry dropped the wedding ring, only to see it stick to an auto tire as a car went by. Hopping on the rear of the car, he made a series of futile attempts to regain the ring with a jackknife as the car went down the street. When he finally succeeded, the tire was in shreds. As Harry left, he helpfully handed the driver his tire jack with the understated advice, "You're going to need this." The startled driver looked back just as his tire blew into a million pieces.

Reaching the church, Harry was welcomed by all and the ceremony began, but not before Professor McGlum took him aside to give him words of doleful advice. Learning that Harry had taken out a large insurance policy on himself, payable to his soon-to-be-wife, McGlum set about planting seeds of doubt. He soon convinced the wide-eyed Harry that he didn't really want to get married after all. On his way out a side door, Harry ran into his prospective father-in-law (William McCall). Forced to go through with the ceremony, Harry perked up when the minister asked if anyone objected to the marriage. No objections came, and this avenue of escape was closed. Next, Harry conveniently "lost" the ring by tossing it over his shoulder. The ring landed in a glass of water. Then, when the bride-to-be fainted, poor Harry tried to revive her with the water, and the mystery was solved.

After the ceremony, Harry got into the wrong car and was on his way to a honeymoon with the wrong bride. Returning to the church, he was unceremoniously thrown into the right automobile by his new wife, and away they went to their home, into which her whole family, including McGlum, had moved. Several ticklish moments followed when Harry's friend convinced him that the drinks being served at the table were poisoned. Leaving together, Harry and McGlum (actually an escaped lunatic) engaged in a wild automobile ride climaxed by a convulsive crash that brought the film to an end.

Filled with choice Langdon bits, *Remember When?* opened with Harry Hudson (Langdon) and Rosemary Lee (Natalie Kingston) as children. Rosemary, leaving town, gave Harry a locket to remember her by. Young Harry then ran away from the orphanage where he was an inmate and headed down life's road. The scene faded out and back in to Harry as a man, trudging along in his oversized coat. A group of tramps being run across the California line by a sheriff interfered with his peaceful existence, Harry barely managing to avoid being knocked down by the horde. Winding up alongside the officer, Harry encouraged him by denouncing the hoboes. Ordered to join them, he moved reluctantly toward them, showing plainly his desire to strike the sheriff. He picked up a stone with the obvious intention of hurling it at the officer's back but dropped it and ran when the sheriff turned to face him.

The scene cut to a circus where Harry's love of many years was working as the bearded lady. Harry, meanwhile, had come upon a momentarily abandoned picnic table loaded with food.

As the hungry Harry picked up one sandwich and started to bite into it, he saw another that looked equally delicious, then another and another. Before he could decide which sandwich he wanted, the picnickers returned, forcing his hasty departure.

Harry next tried to entice some chickens into his clutches, but was foiled by the owner. Harry chanced upon one lone chicken in a doorway, showed it a bread crumb, then put the crumb inside his coat. When he opened his coat, the chicken flew in. Another chicken appeared, and Harry successfully performed the same trick.

A group of hoboes were being questioned by a farmer about the chicken thefts when hapless Harry came along and offered to share his catch. Suspicion turned immediately to him, but he denied being the guilty party. Then a chicken poked its head out from under Harry's coat. Returning the chicken and denying that he had any others, Harry started to explain when a chicken's tail suddenly protruded from behind his pants. Harry's explanation was abruptly ended by the farmer, who gave him a good pummeling, and bird after bird flew out from Harry's clothes.

After a brief episode with some angry bees and on the road again, Harry met Vernon Dent with his circus and was offered a job as handyman. He accepted and tried to climb beneath one of the wagons as if he were riding the rails, but Dent hauled him back up.

In his job as handyman, Harry came on-screen pulling a loaded wagon, but the camera revealed an elephant pushing it for him. Then the elephant helped load a baggage trunk on Harry's shoulders. Harry staggered into a tent with it, dropped the load, and returned, falling to the ground as the beast stepped on him to straighten out his back.

After the third such trip, the elephant picked Harry up and

threw him down. Harry gave the beast such a tongue-lashing that the creature wept elephantine tears. A tender bit of comic action followed as Harry discovered the bearded lady and offered her a cigar. Then he discovered that the circus was across from his old orphanage, a fact which the elated little clown proudly proclaimed to all as the place where "I got my start in life."

The bearded Rosemary sent Harry to the orphanage with a note inquiring what had become of the boy she once knew there. Harry returned with a gang of kids whom he helped sneak into the show, but he was discovered by Dent and fired. On his way out, Harry gave the bearded lady the reply to the note, which informed her of his identity. Shedding her beard, Rosemary was recognized by Harry, and true love was reunited.

Lucky Stars (August 1925) was another laugh-getter with amusing situations and excellent gags expertly utilized by Langdon. Having his horoscope read, Harry learned that he was to take a long journey and meet a dark, beautiful lady. Not waiting for fate, Harry went home and packed, then set out to meet his destiny by boarding a train. While trying to follow his "lucky star," he managed to fall out of the window. As the trip continued, Harry became acquainted with a quack doctor who took his money in return for a promise that he would make Harry a doctor like himself. The two teamed up in a patent medicine business and wandered into a Mexican town. Harry's efforts to make sales afforded some first-rate laughs. Meeting his "dark lady," he made a discovery which was nearly the death of him before the riotous finish—she wore a stiletto in her stocking.

Although washed up in pictures before sound was adopted throughout the industry, Harry, forever planning his big come-back, continued to play whatever roles came his way. They were few and far between, and Langdon fell into the depths of obscurity.[1] Versatile in many fields,[2] he fared as badly in his personal life as in his screen career. He went through five marriages. From 1938 to 1941, he worked as a comedy writer until Monogram signed him for a series of unsuccessful shorts. The little man who once drew a reputed $7,500 a week from Sennett died at the age of sixty, the victim of a cerebral hemorrhage, on December 22, 1944.

One of the early Sennett comedians who has been too often overlooked is Chester Conklin. Born January 11, 1886, Chester grew up in Oskaloosa, the coal-mining district of Iowa. Conklin's success story is a familiar one. His father was a deeply religious man, and he cherished the thought that one day his son would enter the ministry. Chester had different ideas about his future.

Each New Year's Day, the Welsh miners organized a community singing festival in which all of the various singing societies competed at the local Opera House. Chester, who loved each Friday when the class recited aloud, was provided an elocution teacher by his father. The teacher prepared the lad for the New Year's program with a reading of "How Ruby Played," a farmer's impression and description of the piano playing of the great Rubinstein.

When he walked out on the stage before the assembled townspeople, a wonderful and magical feeling came over Chester. This was the life he had dreamed of, and now it was just within his reach. Summoning all of his courage, a bit hesitant at first, he began. Within a short time, he felt perfectly at ease and put everything he had into his delivery. The reading was a tremendous success, and Chester won first prize easily. From that point

[1] He signed with Hal Roach in mid-1929 for a series of talking shorts which failed to restore him to his former fame.

[2] Harry could play almost any musical instrument by ear, was a talented ventriloquist, and once turned down an offer to do a cartoon series for the Hearst newspapers because he was "too busy."

on, he was determined to become a comedian, even if he had to run away from home. He knew his father disapproved of his ambition and felt that if the lad persisted he would be doomed to Hell. But leaving home, family, and father's cherished dreams behind, Chester set out to make his fortune.

It was rough at first, and he quickly discovered that the world at large was not so quick to recognize and appreciate talent as his home town. Sometimes selling papers for a living, sometimes bell-hopping in hotels, Chester did practically anything to support himself while seeking the key to open the locked doors of success. His luck changed in St. Louis when he was employed by a Dutch baker named Schultz. Although he worked hard during the day, Chester had his evenings free. To shorten a dreary evening, he often went to the local vaudeville houses for entertainment, and one night caught the popular act of Weber and Fields. Chester went away grumbling that he could do that act himself.

Weber and Fields performed a German comedy act, the impersonation requiring a blond skullcap wig of closely cropped hair along with a small chin piece. Chester realized that this make-up was typical of the German and Dutch imitators[3] but wondered about the advisability of looking like all other Dutch impersonators. After all, his employer, Schultz, was a Dutchman, but he had a bushy moustache, not at all like the common handlebar type then in vogue. His was more like a brush. Chester decided to use Schultz as his model, adopted a brush moustache, and sat down to write a monologue.

Armed with these tools of the trade, Conklin broke into vaudeville and spent the next few years traveling around the country with both vaudeville acts and stock companies. While playing

[3] Such make-up was popular with stage and screen audiences until World War I, when it fell into disfavor and disuse.

San Francisco, he learned about the L. G. Barnes Wild Animal Circus, which was wintering in Venice. Chester took time off to go to Venice, where he approached Barnes for a job as a clown. During those days, he sang a little refrain in his act: "Heinz, Heinz, what's de matter vid Heinz? Heinz's vobbling down de street, vhat's de matter vid Heinz's feet?" Chester used this skit in his audition and was hired to sing in the chorus and to clown on the side for twenty dollars a week with board.

During the winter season, there was little to do except paint stringers for the boards, which Chester did, for he hated to be idle. Traveling with the circus, he often spent his evenings at the increasingly popular movie houses. Familiar with the antics of the Keystone Cops, Conklin decided to ask Mack Sennett for a job. He located the studio and approached Sennett about work. "Are you funny?" Sennett asked. Chester replied that he clowned for L. G. Barnes, and "I'll leave that up to you." Mack's answer was short and simple: "Well, stick around and we'll use you."

Giving up his circus job, Conklin worked part-time for Keystone at three dollars a day, and in 1913 moved to Majestic for a steady six months' work. Returning to Keystone after that stint, he remained with Sennett for more than six years, and the two became good friends. Chester worked in both one- and two-reelers with the gang, but before leaving the company for good, he was featured in many comedy shorts. Beginning as one of the Cops, Conklin learned his pantomime from one of the best, Ford Sterling. Sterling was patient with the young comedian and helped him develop a pantomimic character in keeping with his appearance. They soon became warm friends.

Chester's best-remembered work at Keystone was in support of Charlie Chaplin and in the "Ambrose-Walrus" series with Mack Swain. He retained his vaudeville costume intact, from baggy pants to brush beard. Generally, his roles called for one

170

of two characterizations: either Droppington, the fumbling, bumbling, mild-mannered little fellow who was always in trouble (as in *A One Night Stand*, March, 1915), or Walrus, the mischievous little imp, the devil incarnate in a five foot, four and one-half inch frame. He utilized the latter characterization in *Love, Speed, and Thrills*, a Keystone of January, 1915, in which he stole his benefactor's wife, and in *Curses! They Remarked* (November, 1914), a burlesque on the old story of a grasping lawyer who passed himself off as the legal guardian of a young orphan girl. As the phony guardian's son, Chester believed that he had the inside track on her affections. When she firmly rejected his attentions, he went out of his way to make life miserable for her. His unwelcome advances were rewarded at the end with a flying crash through the walls of a bedroom with a motorcycle and sidecar.

The life of a circus clown had been a difficult one, but it was ideal preparation for the life of a Keystone comedian. Conklin was called upon to perform many dangerous stunts on the screen, but these sequences were carefully planned. Every now and then, a small mishap would occur, but if the stunts were done with a sense of timing and confidence, the risk was considerably reduced.

Such was the case in the production of *The Cannon Ball* (June, 1915), which used trick photography. Cannon balls chased men or floated serenely over the city with policemen behind them. Chester had no peer when it came to burlesquing the melodramatic villain. As Inspector of High Explosives, he visited a factory and met with the owner and his daughter. While inspecting the powder factory, he horrified employees as he casually tossed cigarets and matches all over the place. He made several unsuccessful plays for the daughter.

During the filming of *The Cannon Ball*, Chester was supposed to be blown from a huge water tank by a controlled explosion. The explosion was premature, sending Conklin flying high into the air. Although he was severely shaken, his presence of mind saved him. Keystoners were expected to be prepared for the unexpected. Even though the studio was flooded with water from the broken tank, the crew went back to work. Sennett's comedians were used to water, and, besides, the broken tank provided a new twist for comic action.

Although many of his fellow workers were often not as fortunate, Conklin suffered only one injury in his long career, and that occurred not on set but during a charity baseball game for the Red Cross in World War I. The bases were wooden blocks anchored by large lag bolts. Chester bunted the ball, then picked it up and put it into his pocket for laughs as he took off for first base. Wallace Reid, on first base, slammed him down and the head of the lag bolt cut into Chester's knee. The mishap incapacitated Conklin for three weeks.

In 1920, Chester was approached by Hampton Del Ruth, then producing Sunshine Comedies for Fox. Del Ruth offered him $500 a week on a contract basis. Although this was $200 more a week than he was receiving from Keystone, Chester replied that he felt he owed allegiance to Keystone, provided Sennett would raise his salary in a new contract. Del Ruth agreed to wait. Cornering Mack on the last day of his contract—which also happened to be pay day—Chester began:

"Mack, listen, my contract is up and I want to talk to you about it."

"Well, go talk to my manager, Mr. Waldron."

"No, I don't know Waldron. I know you and I want to talk to you about it."

"I haven't got time to talk to you."

"You mean by that that you *won't* talk to me?"

"Yes sir."

"All right."

Sennett was a great guy, but he could be tough. So could Chester. He went to his dressing room, packed up his belongings, picked up his check, and drove over to the Fox studios to sign their contract. Monday morning, he began work on the Fox lot. Two days later, a staff member told Sennett: "Chester's over making Sunshines at Fox."

"What are you talking about?"

"He is, he's over there at Fox."

"Like hell he is!"

"He is, you call up and find out."

Sennett picked up the phone and blew sky high. One of his best comedians had flown the coop unbeknownst to him because of his high-handed refusal to spend a few minutes discussing business.

Chester was starred in the Fox comedies and continued to develop a screen character of his own. But it was his misfortune to be overshadowed early in his career by Chaplin, a man whom he admired greatly and whose name was to become a part of the language. Mention of Chester's name today usually brings forth the response, "Oh yes, the little fellow who played with Charlie Chaplin."

Conklin's screen personality had begun more or less as a second banana or foil for others, and second bananas seldom become top bananas. Chester was no exception. His salary was better while at Fox, but his work did not attract the attention his Sennett comedies had received. Many Sunshine comedies were made, but the product as a whole lacked the finesse and polish of the Sennett establishment. Although his pay rose to $750 a week before the silent period ended, Conklin's star rose no further. Had he remained in the Sennett stable, it is possible that the twenties might have seen a blossoming of his popularity, as was the case with Billy Beven and Ben Turpin.

Early in his career, Chester had attended drama classes at night. Like many comedians, he longed to do comedy relief in feature productions. The pay was better, and the work was not nearly as strenuous as turning out a steady stream of short subjects. After leaving Fox, he went to Standard Cinema for a dozen Blue Ribbon comedies in 1925–26. Following these, he teamed with Hank Mann to make a series of two-reel comedies for Tennek Film Corporation with release by International Distributors during 1926–27. He then free-lanced at Universal and Metro-Goldwyn-Mayer before signing his last silent contract with Paramount, where he and W. C. Fields teamed up. His earlier ambition to make people laugh was fulfilled. Chester continued to work through the sound era up until 1960, when he left the screen for good after forty-eight years.

Of all the unsightly comedians ever to work under the Sennett banner, the most outrageous in appearance was the ludicrous scarecrow, Ben Turpin. Ben, more than any other funnyman on the lot, kept Sennett solvent after the departure of Chaplin and Arbuckle for greener pastures. His ability to reduce the conventions of society to an absurd shambles was the mark of his comic genius. His key to success was his eyes. All of the great comedians had a gimmick—Arbuckle, his size; Keaton, his stone face; Chaplin, his tramp; Lloyd, his glasses, and so on. Turpin's "gimmick" was a pair of eyes that were wonderfully, hilariously, unforgettably, and genuinely crossed.

Information on Turpin's early life is extremely difficult to verify, for he, like many of the fine clowns of the silent screen, has been badly neglected by film historians. Theodore Huff, however, sets his birth in New Orleans in 1874. The son of a confectionery storekeeper of French extraction, Ben retained a slight accent throughout his life. At the age of seven, his family moved to New York City, where they took up residence on the lower East Side.

The traditional story is that when Turpin reached his late teens, his father gave him one hundred dollars. The money had been carefully and painfully saved for the time when Ben could leave home with enough money to get him a decent start in life. Ben accepted the nest egg and set off in high spirits but made it only to Jersey City, where he lost everything in a crap game. Afraid to go home, he hopped a freight train that eventually took him to Chicago. Asking a group of tramps gathered around a campfire for advice about how to subsist in the Windy City without food or money, he was told to try "the back door." Turpin's eyes had not yet developed the placement that would bring him fame, and he was a fine-looking man. He managed to live rather well on handouts from Chicago housewives—so well, in fact, that he became a hobo for a while.

Fortunately for millions of people, he realized that this was not how he wanted to spend the rest of his life. A natural comedian, he decided to become an actor, an occupation which many people at the time regarded as only a cut above that of a hobo. Picking up a partner, Ben rehearsed a comedy skit and landed a twenty-dollar-a-week booking for the team. When the partnership broke up, Turpin developed a routine around the character of "Happy Hooligan." With it he rose to a billing in Sam T. Jack's theater (then a popular Chicago burlesque theater), and played the routine on the road for many years.

At this point I think I should correct a few errors which have been perpetuated through the years. Turpin was one of the first slapstick comedians. Shortly after Gilbert M. Anderson and George K. Spoor formed Essanay, Ben was hired, and performed for the camera for about two years (when he was not sweeping the studio floors). His best-remembered effort during this time was *Midnight Disturbance* (1909). His success was limited, and he toured again in the role of "Happy Hooligan," only to reappear on the Essanay lot in 1914. By this time his eyes were permanently crossed, and he had his gimmick. The only problem was how to use it.

How his eyes came to rest where they did has been the subject of many stories. It has been said that he crossed his eyes so many times in his act that one day they stuck that way. Some people asserted that he was injured during a comic fall and his crossed eyes were the curious result; others said it was an accident off the set. One story, whose accuracy may be questioned, had it that his eyes became crossed from watching so many pretty chorus girls. However it came about, Turpin later insured his crossed eyes with Lloyds of London.

He often combined his ocular ability with a "108." A "108" in the trade meant a somersault from a standing start. In Ben's version he did not land on his feet as other comedians did. As the man who always did everything wrong, he was forever making audiences cringe by falling on his face, head, or some other part of his five-foot, four-inch body.

Turpin gained notice as Chaplin's foil in *His New Job* and *A Night Out* (February, 1915). Although Chaplin received the raves, Turpin was noticed, too, and soon he was on his way. During this second stint with Essanay, Ben had once more been assigned janitorial duties, and until the Chaplin pictures came along, he had seriously considered leaving again. Turpin was not given star billing or an opportunity to star while at Essanay. Working with his wife Carrie, whom he had married in 1907, Ben appeared in several one- and two-reel films for the firm. Some were copyrighted and some were not, which makes them difficult to track down today. However, it is known that he was featured in the *Bloggie* and the *Snakeville* series.[4] Warner Brothers re-released many of these in 1920–21.

His next stop was at Vogue in 1916. The history of Vogue and Turpin's tenure there discounts the story which Sennett and Cameron Shipp began in *King of Comedy*, and which many serious writers on the cinema have since adhered to—that is, that Turpin was the first comedian at Keystone to receive the classic pie in the face. Turpin did not arrive at Keystone until after his Vogue contract expired, and by then the pie-throwing gag had been a Sennett staple for years, even appearing in Chaplin's *Caught in a Cabaret* (April, 1914). Evidently Sennett's memory failed him.

The Vogue comedies were nothing out of the ordinary, nor did they utilize Turpin to the best possible advantage. Although he had somewhat refined his style as a result of working with Chaplin, his stint with Vogue produced much the same type of zany, rapid, slapstick films he had made at Essanay. Any comic who could take a fall could make this type of screen comedy. The major difference between the Essanay and Vogue comedies as far as Turpin was concerned was that the latter elevated him to the status of featured comedian. But it was not until after he reached the Sennett studio that his particular comedy style and character evolved, to be accentuated by the lengthy close-ups of his expressive eyes. This accounts to a great extent for his particular identification with Sennett. His earlier work has been forgotten or ignored for the most part; without his association with the Comedy King, he would most likely never have broken out of the ranks of the minor comedians.

From Ben's time with Sennett came some of the finest visual

---

[4] *Countess Bloggie, Bloggie's Vacation, Snakeville's Hen Medic, Snakeville's Champion, Snakeville's Debutantes* were some of the titles of films in which he appeared in supporting roles.

comedies ever made. His first starring role, *A Clever Dummy* (July, 1917) was a marvel of satire. Turpin was always at ease with even the most ridiculous plot, as in *She Loved Him Plenty* (August, 1918). This two-reeler opened with Ben and Charles Lynn as two conscientious pawnshop clerks. They quietly and efficiently began their morning by slightly burning and wetting down a pile of clothes on the counter—as if it were the normal and natural thing to do—before hanging out a "Fire Sale" sign. Marie Prevost and Edgar Kennedy added to the fun in supporting roles.

Turpin was featured in a series of burlesques on popular stage plays during 1919. *East Lynne with Variations* (February) and *Salome vs. Shenendoah* (October) were laugh riots, but the classic was *Uncle Tom Without the Cabin* (August). The camera focused on the stage play as it was presented—or rather as the cast *attempted* to present it. The audience's reaction to what happened on stage was also shown, and in some ways this was nearly as funny as Turpin's portrayal of Uncle Tom. Charles Lynn played Simon Legree, and shapely Marie Prevost was Eliza. Marie managed to display her well-formed figure by losing most of her clothing in the famous ice-crossing scene. The second reel ended with the actors giving living reproductions of famous statues that "brought the house down" wherever this Paramount comedy played.

A Small Town Idol (April, 1921) was a six-reel masterpiece of burlesque on Hollywood that is still recalled today. *Bright Eyes* (January, 1922) contained two classic moments. When Ben innocently stopped to look at a huge clock to get the time of day, the clock broke. When he sat down at the dressing table to brush his hair, the mirror shattered.

As the twenties wore on, Ben turned to more absurd satire

and outrageous burlesque, as in his travesty on *Romeo and Juliet* (August, 1924), which gave critics and Shakespearean devotees a new view of the bard's famous work. As Rodney St. Clair, he reduced Erich von Stroheim to rubble in *A Harem Knight* (November, 1926) and *The Pride of Pikeville* (June, 1927). Strutting and swaggering in his white uniform and black boots, with monocle and walking stick, Turpin faced both danger and beautiful women alike with his rolling eyes and twittering moustache, while his Adam's apple pumped with emotion.

As *The Shriek of Araby* (June, 1923), Ben cut Valentino down to size. Portraying a theater employee who wore a Shiek's costume to advertise the film, Ben was shanghaied and taken to a foreign shore, where he fell into the hands of Arabs. His life was spared by the Shiek, who was leaving on vacation and needed a replacement. Delighted to officiate in the absence of the ruler, Ben took over and immediately captured an artist (Katherine McGuire) painting pictures in the desert. At first she hated him, but Ben applied himself to teaching her the art of love, and what woman could resist Turpin in all of his glory?

Acquiring a magician, Turpin decided to go fishing and the magician's wand provided a lake. Then the two were chased by a lion across the desert until the magician provided a ladder for them to climb up to safety. A wave of the wand turned the lion into a harmless little black cat at their feet. "Why didn't you do that before?" asked the exasperated Shriek. "I couldn't think what I wanted to turn him into," replied the magician. As one might expect, this feature was filled with the trick photography and ingenious sets that Sennett used so often during the twenties. Many amusing touches were added, such as the telephone in a tent, with Ben calling 1492 Pyramid as he read *The Daily Camel*. Had the parody been done in a more subtle manner, it could have been even funnier; nonetheless, the sure comic touch of its director, Richard Jones, insured it as one of Turpin's best-remembered efforts.

Yukon Jake (June, 1924) was typical of Turpin's burlesques on westerns. Ben played Sheriff Cyclone Bill, scourge of bandits, horse thieves, and assorted rustlers. As the film opened, Ben rode into town to find it menaced by bad men. Utilizing his scattergun (a machine gun mounted on the rear of his horse), Turpin effectively shot up the town, to the amusement of his targets, but to the dismay of the townspeople. When the villains rode out of town, they took his sweetheart as hostage. Vowing to bring her back alive, Turpin outfitted himself for the journey with a fur hat and coat.

Using the split-screen technique, he stepped from the right side of the picture (marked "South of '36") to the left side ("North of '36") and found himself in the frozen north. Acquiring a dog team from who knows where, he set off in hot pursuit. A small dog whose feet did not touch the ground was placed in the middle of the team for comic effect. Plunging over a hillside, Ben became a human snowball (done by cartoon animation techniques) and hit against a tree at the bottom of the slope. As he lay stretched out on the ground unconscious, the Sennett Bathing Girls appeared dressed in skimpy furs and placed their igloos in a circle around him. This bit of absurdity had nothing to do with the film proper, but was meant to be interpreted as a dream. As one of the girls bent down to kiss Turpin, he awoke to find a bear licking his face. Turpin at long last came face to face with Yukon Jake (Kalla Pasha) and, with some final nonsense, he rescued the girl and returned a hero.

In July of 1925, Turpin announced his intention to quit the screen, explaining that the serious illness of his wife, Carrie, made his retirement necessary. Friends said that he had to do his own housework because she became irritated with the servants when he was not close by. Carrie had lost her hearing in 1923. In an effort to help her regain it, the Turpins, both devout Catholics, journeyed to the shrine of St. Anne de Beaupré, near her birthplace in Quebec. Their hopes were not realized. Beginning in December, 1924, Carrie suffered from strokes of paralysis, and her death came on October 1 of the next year. Her entire estate, amounting to about $63,000, was left to Ben. The next month, he entered a Santa Barbara hospital for an operation for acute appendicitis. While recovering from the operation, Ben met Babette E. Dietz of Bismarck, North Dakota, a nurse in the hospital. They were married on July 7, 1926. She was to survive him at his death in 1940.

Turpin went back to work again soon after this marriage, for he could not stand the inactivity. He had qualms about not working and earning money, although he really did not need it. At the height of his career, he earned a reputed $3,000 a week. Much of what he earned, he saved or invested. Real estate was his specialty, and the appreciation of rents from his apartment buildings was tremendous. At one time, he made the vow that he would never want for the needed things in life. In the thirties, rumors that he was broke were passed around. Turpin's reply was to spend $50,000 for real estate, paying cash at a time when cash was hard to come by.

As Gerald Montague in *A Blonde's Revenge* (December, 1926), Ben campaigned for the Senate on a platform of less work and more play. His rival was a "reformed" radio announcer who sought to destroy the public faith in Montague by planting his own stenographer in Ben's lap and then snapping pictures. Of course, Ben turned the tables before the end arrived. Garbed in

seaman's clothes, he was a riot in *Broke in China* (April, 1927).
In a Chinese restaurant, Ben related the sad story of his life to
two women.

In 1927, Turpin left Sennett to play a small supporting role in
A Woman's Way,[5] a Columbia release, before retiring more or
less permanently, returning only for cameo roles and only if the
producer met his financial demand of $1,000 a week. His last film
was *Saps at Sea*, the 1940 Laurel and Hardy feature. His role was
minor; he portrayed a janitor whose impaired vision caused him
to connect electrical gadgets in a bizarre fashion.

Ben seldom got along with his directors. He was always at
odds with them and always had his own ideas how a scene should
be played. W. C. Fields discovered how to keep him quiet. Ben's
greatest asset was his crossed eyes, and he lived in mortal fear of
their becoming normal again. He was also, as has been said,
deeply religious. Utilizing these two factors, Fields came up with
the perfect squelch: Whenever Ben began to vent his spleen on
a director, all the director had to say was, "Ben, if you don't see
it my way, I'll go home tonight and pray to St. Joseph to uncross
your eyes," and Turpin became as easy to work with as a con-
tented housecat for as long as three weeks at a stretch.

He was, however, always willing to provide a laugh for a
good cause. In 1927, Atlantic City was the scene of a massive
pre-council parade of Shriners. It was the meeting place for the
fifty-third annual gathering of the Shrine Imperial Council. In
the middle of the afternoon, a small, skinny man dressed in the
uniform of the city police replaced the policeman on duty at the
corner of Tennessee and Atlantic avenues. The replacement was
dressed in a bulky uniform that would have been more suitable
for Fatty Arbuckle. Directing traffic, the man was soon recog-

[5] He had previously played a supporting role in Monte Blue's Warner feature, *Hogan's Alley* (1925).

nized, and as the name "Ben Turpin" spread, the number of cars using the street grew. Shortly, the corner became the scene of one of the worst traffic jams the city had ever witnessed. The more Ben attempted to straighten the situation out, the worse it became.

Stymied, and after a great deal of frantic arm waving, he threw up his hands in despair. Walking over to a roadster, Ben arrested the pretty young woman driver and climbed into the car. He ordered her to drive to police headquarters, and more than one hundred cars followed, carrying the traffic disturbance across the city. At headquarters, the young woman insisted that she had done nothing wrong. "She did," Ben interrupted. "She wouldn't go where I was looking." The charge was dismissed, of course, and the chief of police accepted Turpin's resignation from the force.

Ben Turpin's career practically spanned the silent period, and he created many comedy classics of enduring value. A fine acrobat, he was able to take many severe falls late into his fifties. A slapstick artist of the finest variety, his forte was broad pantomime and low comedy.

All through the twenties, Sennett's affairs continued to prosper. Eight hundred thousand dollars had been expended in the construction of a new lot in Studio City. It was completed in time to be used in making the 1927–28 releases. These amounted to thirty-six double reels evenly divided among the Sennett comedies, the "Smith Family" series, and the Sennett Girl comedies. The Sennett comedies provided a showcase for Billy Bevan, Andy Clyde, and Jack Cooper. The "Smith Family" series had found favor with audiences because of Raymond McKee's own unique brand of humor and Ruth Hiatt's good looks. The real star of these comedies was perhaps little Mary Ann Jackson, whose abilities as an actress were on a par with those of any of the child stars of the time. Her saucy looks and actions brought many laughs, and she and her animal friends contributed much to the humor. The Sennett Girl comedies featured Daphne Pollard and Dot Farley for comic relief, along with all of the bathing beauties. In 1928 the public got its first glimpse of these bathing beauties in Technicolor in *The Swim Princess*.

When Sennett's contract with Pathé came up for renewal in 1928, a deadlock occurred. The short subject market was in a slump, and Pathé did not immediately agree with the master on the value of his product. While waiting for Pathé to come around, Sennett canceled all contracts, except for two of his more promising newcomers, Johnny Burke and Sally Eilers. Pathé was beset with internal problems at the time and no solution appeared to be in sight. With the future of silent films doubtful, Sennett, in preparation for the 1929–30 season, changed his studio over to the RCA Photophone process and arranged to market his release schedule through Educational. An era had ended.

By 1930 the silent motion picture comedy short was on its way out. Many of its practitioners found a difficult future ahead of them. Chaplin was at work on *City Lights*, which he decided to release as a silent. Harold Lloyd's best work had been done, but he was to be fairly successful in making the transition from silents to sound, as were Laurel and Hardy. Buster Keaton was ruined by dialogue, which broke the spell cast by his stone-faced appearance. Harry Langdon was finished, Ben Turpin had retired, and Larry Semon was dead.

A new group of comics became the vanguard in the short motion picture sound comedies. Andy Clyde, Eddie Quillan, Edgar Kennedy, W. C. Fields, and Charlie Chase had had experience in the silent medium, but their talents came to full flower in the thirties. The two-reel comedy short might possibly have recouped its strength and gone on, but the public's enthusiasm for sound and its acceptance of the cartoons and double features dealt a fatal blow to the silent comedy short; it died a lingering death. With the advent of sound, a unique form of motion picture entertainment passed from the scene, never to return.

Selected Comedians and Their Films

In the following pages, certain comedians have been singled out and their works compiled for reference. Every attempt has been made to provide as accurate and complete a listing of the films of each comic or team as possible. Each listing contains all of the silent films made by a particular comedian or those films up through 1929, including talking or part-talking pictures for that year. The list includes: Billy Bevan, Charlie Chaplin, Buster Keaton, Harry Langdon, Stanley Laurel, Laurel and Hardy, Harold Lloyd, "Our Gang," Snub Pollard, Larry Semon, Ben Turpin.

The Comedies of Billy Bevan

Bevan made many unbilled appearances in L-KO comedies and is found in small supporting roles in a number of the Sennett comedies of 1919. This index begins with his leading roles, all of which were done for Sennett in two reels with the exception of appearances in two features.

	1920	*Directed by*
May	*Let'Er Go*	James Davis
July	*The Quack Doctor*	George Gray and Bevan
September	*It's A Boy*	Noel Smith
October	*My Goodness*	Noel Smith
November	*Love, Honor and Behave* (5 reels)	F. Richard Jones and Erle Kenton
November	*A Fireside Brewer*	Noel Smith

	1921	
February	*A Small Town Idol* (7 reels)	Erle Kenton
December	*Be Reasonable*	Roy Del Ruth
	By Heck	Roy Del Ruth
July	*Astray from the Steerage*	Frank Powell

	1922	
February	*The Duck Hunter*	Roy Del Ruth
March	*On Patrol*	F. Richard Jones
April	*Oh Daddy*	Roy Del Ruth
May	*Gymnasium Jim*	F. Richard Jones
June	*Ma And Pa*	Roy Del Ruth
November	*When Summer Comes*	Roy Del Ruth

	1923	
August	*Nip and Tuck*	Roy Del Ruth
December	*Inbad The Sailor*	Erle Kenton

	1924	
January	*One Spooky Night*	
August	*Wall Street Blues*	
September	*Lizzies of the Field*	Del Lord
October	*Wandering Waistlines*	
November	*The Cannon Ball Express*	Del Lord

1925

January	*Honeymoon Hardships*	Tom Garnett and Jefferson Moffitt
March	*Giddap*	Del Lord
April	*The Lion's Whiskers*	Del Lord
May	*Skinners in Silk*	Del Lord
June	*Super-Hooper-Dyne Lizzies*	Del Lord
July	*Sneezing Beezers*	Del Lord
August	*The Iron Nag*	Del Lord
	Butter Fingers	Del Lord
October	*Over There-Abouts*	
December	*From Rags To Britches*	

1926

January	*Whispering Whiskers*	Del Lord
February	*Trimmed in Gold*	
March	*Circus Today*	Lloyd Bacon
	Wandering Willies	Del Lord
April	*Hayfoot, Strawfoot*	Gil Pratt and Jefferson Moffitt
May	*Fight Night*	Gil Pratt
	Muscle Bound Music	Alf Goulding
June	*Ice Cold Cocos*	Del Lord
July	*A Sea Dog's Tale*	Del Lord
August	*Hubby's Quiet Little Game*	Del Lord
September	*Hoboken to Hollywood*	Del Lord
October	*Masked Mamas*	
November	*The Divorce Dodger*	Del Lord
December	*Flirty Four-Flushers*	Eddie Cline

1927

January	*Should Sleepwalkers Marry?*	
February	*Peaches and Plumbers*	
March	*A Small Town Princess*	
May	*The Bull Fighter*	Earle Rodney

June	*Cured in the Excitement*	Earle Rodney
September	*The Golf Nut*	Harry Edwards
October	*Gold Digger of Weepah*	Harry Edwards

1928

January	*The Beach Club*	Harry Edwards
February	*The Best Man*	Harry Edwards
March	*The Bicycle Flirt*	Harry Edwards
August	*His Unlucky Night*	Harry Edwards
September	*Caught in the Kitchen*	"Tired Business-man's" series directed by Phil Whitman
	Motorboat Mamas	Harry Andrews
October	*Motoring Mamas*	Phil Whitman
November	*Hubby's Latest Alibi*	Phil Whitman
December	*Hubby's Weekend Trip*	Harry Edwards
	The Lion's Roar (all-talking and released through Educational under Sennett's contract following his break with Pathé)	
	His New Steno	Phil Whitman

1929

February	*Calling Hubby's Bluff*	Harry Edwards
	Button My Back	Phil Whitman
March	*Foolish Husbands*	Phil Whitman
April	*Pink Pajamas*	Phil Whitman
June	*Don't Get Jealous*	

THE COMEDIES OF CHARLIE CHAPLIN

Listed below are the original titles of Chaplin's films in the order in which they were released, along with the various other names which accompanied their re-release. A more detailed listing is given in the index of Theodore Huff's *Charlie Chaplin* (Schuman, 1951), a volume no cinema addict should overlook.

1914—For Keystone (One reel unless otherwise indicated)

February   *Making a Living (A Busted Johnny, Troubles, Doing His Best)*

Kid Auto Races at Venice (split-reel)

Mabel's Strange Predicament (The Hotel Mix-up)

Between Showers (The Flirts, In Wrong, Charlie and the Umbrella)

March   *A Film Johnnie (The Movie Nut, The Million Dollar Job)*

Tango Tangles (Charlie's Recreation, The Music Hall)

His Favorite Pastime (The Bonehead)

Cruel, Cruel Love (Lord Help Us)

April   *The Star Boarder (The Hash-House Hero)*

Mabel at the Wheel (2 reels) *(His Daredevil Queen, A Hot Finish)*

Twenty Minutes of Love (He Loved Her So, Cops and Watches, The Love-Friend)

Caught in a Cabaret (2 reels) *(The Waiter, The Jazz Waiter, Faking with Society)*

May   *Caught in the Rain (At It Again, Who Got Stung?, In the Park)*

A Busy Day (split-reel) *(The Militant Suffragette)*

June   *The Fatal Mallet (The Pile Driver)*

Her Friend the Bandit (Mabel's Flirtation)

The Knockout (2 reels) *(Counted Out, The Pugilist)*

Mabel's Busy Day (Charlie and the Sausages, Love and Lunch, Hot Dogs)

July   *Laughing Gas (Turning His Ivories, The Dentist, Down and Out)*

August   *The Property Man* (2 reels) *(The Roustabout, Getting His Goat)*

The Face on the Barroom Floor (The Ham Artist)

The Masquerader (Putting One Over, The Picnic, The Female Impersonator, The New Janitor)

Recreation (split-reel) *(Spring Fever)*

His New Profession (The Good-for-Nothing, Helping Himself)

September *The Rounders (Revelry, Two of a Kind, Oh, What a Night)*

The New Janitor (The New Porter, The Blundering Boob)

October *Those Love Pangs (The Rival Mashers, Busted Hearts)*

Dough and Dynamite (2 reels) *(The Doughnut Designer, The Cook)*

Gentlemen of Nerve (Some Nerve)

November *His Musical Career (The Piano Movers, Musical Tramps)*

His Trysting Place (2 reels) *(The Family House)*

Tillie's Punctured Romance (6 reels)

December *Getting Acquainted (A Fair Exchange)*

His Prehistoric Past (2 reels) *(A Dream)*

1915—For Essanay (two reels unless otherwise indicated)

February *His New Job*

  A Night Out

March *The Champion*

In the Park (1 reel)

April *The Jitney Elopement*

The Tramp

By the Sea (1 reel)

June *Work (The Paperhanger)*

July *A Woman (The Perfect Lady, Charlie and the Perfect Lady)*

August *The Bank (Charlie at the Bank)*

| October | *Shanghaied* |
| November | *A Night in the Show* |

1916

March	*Police*
April	*Carmen* (4 reels)
August	*Triple Trouble*
September	*The Essanay—Chaplin Revue of 1916* (5 reels) (Contained scenes from *His New Job, A Night Out,* and *The Tramp.* A similar compilation entitled *Chase Me Charlie* in seven reels was released in England in May, 1918, by George Kleine.)

1916—For Mutual (all were two reels)

May	*The Floorwalker*
June	*The Fireman*
July	*The Vagabond*
August	*One A.M.*
September	*The Count*
October	*The Pawnshop*
November	*Behind the Screen*
December	*The Rink*

1917

January	*Easy Street*
April	*The Cure*
June	*The Immigrant*
October	*The Adventurer*

1918—For First National

| April | *A Dog's Life* (3 reels) |
| October | *Shoulder Arms* (3 reels) (A split-reel entitled *The Bond* was also made by Chaplin for the war effort and was in distribution during the autumn of 1918.) |

1919

| June | *Sunnyside* (3 reels) |

December   *A Day's Pleasure* (2 reels)

1921
February   *The Kid* (6 reels)
September   *The Idle Class* (2 reels)

1922
April   *Pay Day* (2 reels)

1923
February   *The Pilgrim* (4 reels)

1923—For United Artists
October   *A Woman of Paris* (Chaplin did not star in this eight-reel film but wrote and directed it as a starring vehicle for Edna Purviance.)

1925
August   *The Gold Rush* (9 reels)

1928
January   *The Circus* (7 reels)

1931
February   *City Lights* (9 reels)

1936
February   *Modern Times* (This, Chaplin's last silent, was released after sound had established itself and was met with mixed reactions. His only concessions to sound were a musical accompaniment, sound effects, and a few spoken sentences which eminated from loud-speakers.)

THE COMEDIES OF BUSTER KEATON

Keaton had prominent roles in the following fifteen Arbuckle-Paramount comedies before going on his own:

1917

Two Reels

April	*The Butcher Boy*
May	*A Reckless Romeo*
June	*The Rough House*
August	*His Wedding Night*
September	*Oh, Doctor!*
October	*Fatty at Coney Island*
December	*A Country Hero*

1918

January	*Out West*
March	*The Bell Boy*
May	*Moonshine*
July	*Good Night Nurse*
September	*The Cook*

1919

September	*Back Stage*
November	*The Hayseed*

1920

January	*The Garage*

In October, Metro Pictures Corporation released the seven-reel feature, *The Saphead*, directed by Herbert Blaché, in which Keaton had a starring role. He then went into a series of two-reel comedies of his own.

Released by Metro

September	*One Week*	Written and directed by Keaton and Eddie Cline
October	*Convict 13*	Keaton and Cline
November	*The Scarecrow*	Keaton and Cline
December	*Neighbors*	Keaton and Cline

1921

February	*The Haunted House*	Keaton and Cline

March	*Hard Luck*	Keaton and Cline
April	*The High Sign*	Keaton and Cline
May	*The Goat*	Written and directed by Keaton and Malcolm St. Clair

Released by Associated First National

October	*The Playhouse*
November	*The Boat*

1922

January	*The Paleface*	
March	*Cops*	
May	*My Wife's Relations*	
July	*The Blacksmith*	Written and directed by Keaton and St. Clair
August	*The Frozen North*	
October	*The Electric House*	
November	*Day Dreams* (3 reels)	

1923

January	*The Balloonatic*
March	*The Love Nest*

Keaton made the following features (released by Metro-Goldwyn-Mayer):

September	*The Three Ages* (6 reels)	Directed by Keaton and Cline
November	*Our Hospitality* (7 reels)	Keaton and Jack Blystone

1924

April	*Sherlock, Jr.* (5 reels)	Keaton
October	*The Navigator* (6 reels)	Keaton and Donald Crisp

1925

March	*Seven Chances* (6 reels)	Keaton
November	*Go West* (7 reels)	Keaton

1926

September	*Battling Butler* (7 reels)	Keaton

1927

February	*The General* (8 reels)	Keaton and Clyde Bruckman (released by United Artists)
September	*College* (6 reels)	James Horn (released by United Artists)

1928

May	*Steamboat Bill, Jr.* (7 reels)	Charles F. Reisner (released by United Artists)
September	*The Cameraman* (8 reels)	Edward Sedgwick (released by M-G-M)

1929

April	*Spite Marriage* (9 reels)	Edward Sedgwick (released by M-G-M)

The Film Quarterly Supplement No. 1 (University of California Press, Berkeley) provides more detailed information, compiled by George Geltzer, on Keaton's films.

THE COMEDIES OF HARRY LANGDON

For Mack Sennett

1924

Two Reels		*Directed by*
February	*Picking Peaches*	Erle Kenton
March	*Smile Please*	Hampton Del Ruth
	Shanghaied Lovers	Roy Del Ruth
April	*Flickering Youth*	Erle Kenton
May	*The Cat's Meow*	Roy Del Ruth
June	*His New Mamma*	Roy Del Ruth
August	*The First Hundred Years*	F. Richard Jones
September	*The Luck O' The Foolish*	Harry Edwards

October	*The Hanson Cabman*	Harry Edwards
November	*All Night Long*	Harry Edwards
December	*Feet of Mud*	Harry Edwards

1925

January	*The Sea Squawk*	Harry Edwards
February	*Boobs In The Woods*	Harry Edwards
March	*His Marriage Wow*	Harry Edwards
	Plain Clothes	Harry Edwards
April	*Remember When?*	Harry Edwards
June	*Horace Greely Jr.*	Alf Goulding
July	*The White Wing's Bride*	Alf Goulding
August	*Lucky Stars*	Harry Edwards
November	*There He Goes* (3 reels)	Harry Edwards

1926

January	*Saturday Afternoon* (3 reels)	Harry Edwards
April	*Fiddlesticks*	Harry Edwards
May	*The Soldier Man* (3 reels)	Harry Edwards

For Hal Roach

Two Reels—Sound   1929

August	*Hotter Than Hot*	Lewis Foster
September	*The Fighting Parson*	Charles Rogers and Fred Guiol
October	*The Sky Boy*	Charles Rogers
November	*Skirt Shy*	Charles Rogers

Langdon also made the following features, produced by the Harry Langdon Film Corporation for release through First National:

1926

Tramp, Tramp, Tramp (6 reels)	Harry Edwards
The Strong Man (7 reels)	Frank Capra

Six reels		1927	
	Long Pants		Frank Capra
	Three's A Crowd		Langdon

		1928	
	The Chaser		Langdon
	Heart Trouble		Langdon

THE COMEDIES OF STAN LAUREL

During 1918–19, Laurel made several appearances in both L-KO and Nestor films, such as *Hickory Hiram* (1 reel, Nestor, released April, 1918), *Phoney Photos* (2 reel, L-KO, released July, 1918), and *It's Great To Be Crazy* (1 reel, Nestor, released December, 1918). These were not well documented and have been lost. Laurel also worked in several Larry Semon comedies such as *Huns and Hyphens, Bears and Bad Men,* and *Frauds and Frenzies,* released consecutively in October, November, and December, 1918. After making five single-reel comedies for Hal Roach's Rolin Flim Company, he went back to vaudeville and began supporting Semon again. This listing begins with his first screen appearances as a leading comedian.

		1922	
Two Reels	For Quality-Metro		Directed by G. M. Anderson
February	*When Knights Were Cold*		
September	*The Egg*		
October	*Weak End Party*		
November	*Mud and Sand*		
December	*The Pest*		
One Reel		For Roach	
May	*White Wings*		Directed by George Jeske

| | | 1923 | |
| *Two Reels* | For Quality-Metro | | |

March	*The Handy Man*	
One Reel	For Roach	
April	*Noon Whistle*	George Jeske
June	*Under Two Jags*	George Jeske
	Pick and Shovel	George Jeske
July	*Collars and Cuffs*	George Jeske
	Kill or Cure	Percy Pembroke
	Gas and Air	Percy Pembroke
August	*Oranges and Lemons*	George Jeske
September	*Short Orders*	
	Man About Town	
	Roughest Africa	Ralph Cedar
October	*Frozen Hearts*	Jay A. Howe
November	*The Whole Truth*	
	Save The Ship	
	The Soilers	Ralph Cedar
December	*Scorching Sands*	
	Mother's Joy	Ralph Cedar

1924

One Reel	For Roach	
January	*The Smithy*	George Jeske
February	*Postage Due*	George Jeske
March	*Zeb vs. Paprika*	Ralph Cedar
April	*Brothers Under the Chin*	Ralph Cedar
May	*Near Dublin*	Ralph Cedar
June	*Rupert of Hee-Haw*	Percy Pembroke
July	*Wide Open Spaces*	George Jeske
August	*Short Kilts*	George Jeske

For Standard Cinema—Selznick

August	*Mandam Mix-Up*	(a series of twelve double
October	*Detained*	reels directed by Joe
December	*Monsieur Don't Care*	Rock and Percy Pem-
	West of Hot Dog	broke)

1925

January	*Somewhere in Wrong*
February	*Twins*
March	*Pie-Eyed*
April	*Snow Hawk*
May	*Navy Blue Days*
June	*The Sleuth*
July	*Dr. Pyckle and Mr. Pride*
August	*Half A Man*

Laurel returned to Hal Roach to write and direct. In 1926 he made three appearances in the Comedy All Star series; the next year was to see the creation of the fabulous team of Laurel and Hardy. His 1926 releases for Roach were: *Atta Boy* and *Get 'Em Young* (October), and *On the Front Page* (November).

THE LAUREL AND HARDY COMEDIES

Stanley Laurel and Oliver Hardy began appearing together in the Hal Roach Comedy All Stars Series. They were not billed as a team until after Roach moved his distribution to M-G-M in late 1927. They clicked at once with audiences and exhibitors and went on to become one of the all-time great comedy teams.

1927—For Pathé

March	*Duck Soup*	The Pathé Comedy All-
April	*Slipping Wives*	Star Series alternated
May	*Eve's Love Letters*	Hal Yates, Fred Guiol,
June	*Love 'Em and Weep*	Clyde Bruckman and
July	*Why Girls Love Sailors*	Frank Butler as direc-
August	*With Love and Hisses*	tors.
September	*Sailors Beware*	
November	*Do Detectives Think?*	

1928—For Pathé

January	*Should Tall Men Marry?*
February	*Flying Elephants*

1927—For M-G-M

September	*Sugar Daddies*	Fred Guiol
October	*Call of the Cuckoo* (a guest appearance)	Clyde Bruckman
	The Second Hundred Years (the first Laurel and Hardy comedy)	Fred Guiol
November	*Hats Off* (Max Davidson and Oliver Hardy were starred with Stan in support)	Hal Yates
December	*Putting Pants on Philip*	Clyde Bruckman
	Battle of the Century	Clyde Bruckman

1928—For M-G-M

January	*Leave 'Em Laughing*	Clyde Bruckman
February	*The Finishing Touch*	Clyde Bruckman
March	*From Soup to Nuts*	Edgar Kennedy
April	*You're Darn Tooting*	Edgar Kennedy
May	*Their Purple Moment*	Fred Guiol
September	*Should Married Men Go Home?* (released in sound and silent versions)	James Parrott
October	*Early To Bed*	Emmett Flynn
November	*Two Tars*	James Parrott
December	*Habeas Corpus*	Leo McCarey
	We Faw Down	Leo McCarey

1929—For M-G-M

January	*Liberty* (silent and sound)	Leo McCarey
February	*Wrong Again* (silent and sound)	
March	*That's My Wife*	Lloyd French
April	*Big Business*	James Horne

May	*Double Whoopee*	Lewis Foster
June	*Berth Marks* (silent and sound)	
	Men O'War (silent and sound)	
August	*A Perfect Day*	James Parrott
September	*They Go Boom*	
October	*Bacon Grabbers*	Lewis Foster
December	*Angora Love*	

The Comedies of Harold Lloyd

All of Lloyd's short comedies were made for Hal Roach and re-leased through Pathé. None of his "Willie Work" comedies reached the market. Beginning in September, 1917, Lloyd alter-nated the Lonesome Luke films with the characterization that was to make him famous, dropping Luke for good at the close of the year. Unless otherwise indicated, his comedies were one reel in length. Lloyd, Roach, and Alf Goulding all had a hand in directing them.

1915

July	*Once Every Ten Minutes*
	Spit Ball Sadie
August	*Soaking the Clothes*
	Pressing His Suit
	Terribly Stuck Up
September	*A Mixup for Mazie*
	Some Baby
October	*Fresh From The Farm*
November	*Giving Them Fits*
	Bughouse Bell Hops
	Tinkering With Trouble
	Great While It Lasted
	Ragtime Snap Shots

December	*A Fozzle at a Tea Party*
	Ruses, Rhymes, Roughnecks
	Peculiar Patients Pranks
	Social Gangster

1916

January	*Luke Leans to the Literary*
	Luke Lugs Luggage
	Luke Rolls in Luxury
	Luke the Candy Cut-Up
February	*Luke Foils the Villain*
	Luke and Rural Roughnecks
March	*Luke Pipes the Pippins*
	Lonesome Luke, Circus King
April	*Skylight Sleep*
	Luke's Double
	Them Was the Happy Days
May	*Trouble Enough*
	Luke and the Bomb Throwers
	Reckless Wrestlers
	Luke's Late Lunches
	Ice
June	*Luke Laughs Last*
	An Awful Romance
	Luke's Fatal Flivver
	Luke's Society Mixup
July	*Luke's Washful Waiting*
	Luke Rides Roughshod
	Unfriendly Fruit
	Luke, Crystal Gazer
	A Matrimonial Mixup
August	*Luke's Lost Lamb*
	Braver Than the Bravest
	Luke Does the Midway
	Caught in a Jam

September	*Luke Joins the Navy*
	Busting the Beanery
	Luke and the Mermaids
	Jailed
October	*Luke's Speedy Club Life*
	Luke and the Bang-Tails
	Luke, the Chauffeur
November	*Luke's Preparedness Preparation*
	Luke, Gladiator
	Luke, Patient Provider
	Luke's Newsie Knockout
December	*Luke's Movie Muddle*
	Luke's Fireworks Fizzle
	Luke Locates the Loot
	Luke's Shattered Sleep

1917

January	*Luke's Last Liberty*
	Luke's Busy Days
	Drama's Dreadful Deal
	Luke's Trolley Trouble
February	*Lonesome Luke, Lawyer*
	Luke Wins Ye Ladye Faire
March	*Lonesome Luke's Lively Rifle*
April	*Lonesome Luke on Tin Can Alley* (2 reels)
May	*Lonesome Luke's Lively Life* (2 reels)
	Lonesome Luke's Honeymoon (2 reels)
June	*Lonesome Luke, Plumber* (2 reels)
July	*Stop! Luke! Listen!* (2 reels)
August	*Lonesome Luke, Messenger* (2 reels)
	Lonesome Luke, Mechanic (2 reels)
September	*Lonesome Luke's Wild Women* (2 reels)
	Over the Fence (Lloyd's first comedy using his new character with glasses. These single reels alternated

with the double-reel "Lukes" until December, when
Lloyd retired the Luke character.)

Lonesome Luke Loses Patients (2 reels)
Pinched
By the Sad Sea Waves

October   *Birds of a Feather* (2 reels)
Bliss
Lonesome Luke from London to Laramie (2 reels)
Rainbow Island

November   *Love, Laughs and Lather* (2 reels)
The Flirt
Clubs Are Trump (2 reels)
All Aboard

December   *We Never Sleep* (2 reels)
Bashful
The Tip
Step Lively

1918

January   *The Big Idea*
The Lamb

February   *Hit Him Again*
Beat It

March   *A Gasoline Wedding*
Look Pleasant Please
Here Come the Girls
Let's Go
On the Jump

April   *Follow the Crowd*
Pipe the Whiskers
It's a Wild Life
Hey There

May   *Kicked Out*
The Non-Stop Kid

Two-Gun Gussie
Fireman, Save My Child
June   *The City Slicker*
Sic 'Em Towser
Somewhere in Turkey
Are Crooks Dishonest?
July   *An Ozark Romance*
Kicking The Germ Out of Germany
August   *That's Him*
September   *Too Scrambled*
Swing Your Partner
October   *Why Pick on Me?*
Nothing But Trouble
December   *Hear 'Em Rave*
Take a Chance
She Loses Me

1919

January   *Wanted—$5000*
Going! Going! Gone!
February   *Ask Father*
On the Fire
March   *I'm On My Way*
Look Out Below
The Dutiful Dub
Next Aisle Over
April   *A Sammy in Siberia*
Just Dropped In
Crack Your Heels
Ring Up the Curtain
May   *Young Mr. Jazz*
Si, Señor
Before Breakfast
The Marathon

June	*Back to the Woods*
	Pistols for Breakfast
	Swat the Crook
	Off the Trolley
	Spring Fever
July	*Billy Blazes, Esq.*
	Just Neighbors
	At the Stage Door
	Never Touched Me
August	*A Jazzed Honeymoon*
	Count Your Change
	Chop Suey & Co.
	Heap Big Chief
	Don't Shove
September	*Be My Wife*
	The Rajah
	He Leads, Others Follow
	Soft Money
October	*Count the Votes*
	Pay Your Dues
November	*Bumping Into Broadway* (2 reels)
	Captain Kidd's Kids (2 reels)
December	*From Hand to Mouth*
	His Royal Slyness

1920

Haunted Spooks   (All 1920 releases were
An Eastern Westerner   two reels in length.)
High and Dizzy
Get Out and Get Under
Number, Please

1921

Now or Never (3 reels)
Among Those Present (3 reels)

I Do (2 reels)
Never Weaken (3 reels)
A Sailor-Made Man   Directed by
   (4 reels)   Fred Newmeyer

Lloyd made the following features for release through Pathé, except where otherwise indicated.

	1922	*Directed by*
Grandma's Boy (5 reels)		Fred Newmeyer
Dr. Jack (6 reels)		Fred Newmeyer

1923
Safety Last (6 reels)   Fred Newmeyer and
                    Sam Taylor

Why Worry? (6 reels)

1924
Girl Shy (8 reels)
Hot Water (5 reels)

1925
The Freshman (7 reels)

1926
For Heaven's Sake   Sam Taylor (released by
   (6 reels)   Paramount)

1927
The Kid Brother (8 reels)   Ted Wilde (released by
                    Paramount)

1928
Speedy (8 reels)   Ted Wilde (released by
                    Paramount)

1929
Welcome Danger   Clyde Bruckman (released
   (12 reels) (This was   by Paramount)
   Lloyd's first sound film.)

The "Our Gang" Comedies

Popular with audiences well into the sound era, the "Our Gang" comedies were profitable for Hal Roach from the beginning. All were made in two reels and often featured guest appearances by other top Roach comics, including Charlie Chase and Snub Pollard. Unless otherwise indicated, the Pathé releases were directed by Robert McGowan.

1922

September	*One Terrible Day*	
October	*Fire Fighters*	
November	*Our Gang* (with Snub Pollard)	
	Young Sherlocks	
December	*Saturday Morning*	
	A Quiet Street	

1923

January	*The Champeen*	
February	*The Cobbler*	Tom McNamara
	The Big Show	
March	*A Pleasant Journey*	
April	*Boys to Board*	Tom McNamara
May	*Giants vs. Yanks*	
June	*Back Stage*	
July	*Dogs of War*	
	Lodge Night	
August	*July Days*	
September	*No Noise*	
October	*Stage Fright*	
November	*Derby Days*	
December	*The Great Outdoors*	
	Sunday Calm	

1924

January	*Tire Trouble*

February	*Big Business*	
March	*The Buccaneers*	Mark Haldane
April	*Seein' Things*	
May	*Commencement Day*	Mark Haldane
June	*Cradle Robbers*	
	Jubilo Jr.	
July	*It's A Bear*	
August	*High Society*	
September	*The Sun Down Limited*	
October	*Every Man for Himself*	
November	*Fast Company*	
December	*The Mysterious Mystery*	

1925

January	*The Big Town*
February	*Circus Fever*
March	*Dog Days*
April	*The Love Bug*
May	*Shootin' Injuns*
	Ask Grandma
June	*Official Officers*
July	*Boys Will Be Joys*
August	*Mary, Queen of Tots*
September	*Your Own Back Yard*
November	*Better Movies*
December	*One Wild Ride*

1926

January	*Good Cheer*
February	*Buried Treasure*
March	*Monkey Business*
April	*Baby Clothes*
May	*Uncle Tom's Uncle*
July	*Thundering Fleas* (with Charlie Chase)
August	*Shivering Spooks*

September	*The Fourth Alarm*	
November	*War Feathers*	Anthony Mack
December	*Telling Whoppers*	Anthony Mack

1927

January	*Bring Home the Turkey*	Anthony Mack
February	*Seeing the World*	Anthony Mack
March	*Ten Years Old*	
April	*Love My Dog*	
May	*The Tired Businessman*	
June	*Baby Brother*	
July	*The Glorious Fourth*	
September	*Olympic Games*	Anthony Mack
November	*Chicken Feed*	Anthony Mack and Charles Oelze

1928

| January | *Playin' Hookey* | Anthony Mack |
| February | *The Smile Wins* | |

Released Through M-G-M
1927

September	*Yale vs. Harvard*	McGowan, Mack, and
October	*The Old Wallop*	Oelze alternated direc-
November	*Heebee Jeebees*	tion of the M-G-M
December	*Dog Heaven*	comedies.

1928

January	*Spook Spoofing*	
February	*Rainy Days*	
March	*Edison, Marconi & Co.*	
April	*Barnum & Ringling, Inc.*	
May	*Fair and Muddy*	
June	*Crazy House*	
September	*Growing Pains*	
October	*Ol' Gray Hoss*	

| November | *School Begins* |
| December | *The Spanking Age* |

1929

January	*Election Day*
February	*Noisy Noises* (released in silent and sound)
March	*Holy Terror*
April	*Wiggle Your Ears*
May	*Fast Freight*
	Small Talk (silent and sound)
June	*Little Mother*
	Railroadin' (silent and sound)
July	*Dad's Day* (silent and sound)
	Boxing Gloves (silent and sound)
August	*Lazy Days*
September	*Cat, Dog and Co.*
October	*Bouncing Babies*
November	*Saturday's Lesson*
December	*Moan and Groan, Inc.*

THE COMEDIES OF SNUB POLLARD

Pollard was one of the busiest comedians on the Roach lot. Prior to being given his own series, he had supported Harold Lloyd from 1915 to 1919. He made more than one hundred single reels and a series of thirteen double reels before producing his own series for the independent market. Unless otherwise indicated, Charles Parrott directed.

1919

October	*Start Something*
November	*All At Sea*
	Call for Mr. Cave Man
	Giving the Bride Away
	Order in Court
	It's a Hard Life

December	*How Dry I Am*
	Looking For Trouble
	Tough Luck
	The Floor Below

1920

January	*Red Hot Hottentots*
	Why Go Home?
	Slippery Slickers
	The Dippy Dentist
February	*All Lit Up*
	Getting His Goat
	Waltz Me Around
	Raise the Rent
	Find the Girl
March	*Fresh Paint*
	Flat Broke
	Cut the Cards
	The Dinner Hour
April	*Cracked Wedding Bells*
	Speed to Spare
	Shoot on Sight
	Don't Weaken
May	*Drink Hearty*
	Trotting Through Turkey
	All Dressed Up
	Grab the Ghost
June	*All in a Day*
	Any Old Port
July	*Don't Rock the Boat*
	The Home Stretch
	Call a Taxi
August	*Live and Learn*
	Run 'Em Ragged

A London Bobby
Money To Burn
September *Go As You Please*
Rock-a-by-Baby
Doing Time
October *Fellow Citizens*
When the Wind Blows
November *Insulting the Sultan*
The Dearly Departed
December *Cash Customers*
Park Your Car

1921

January *The Morning After*
Whirl o' the West
February *Open Another Bottle*
His Best Girl
March *Make It Snappy*
Fellow Romans
April *Rush Orders*
Bubbling Over
May *No Children*
Own Your Own Home
Big Game
Save Your Money
June *Blue Sunday*
Where's the Fire
The High Rollers
July *You're Next*
The Bike Bug
At the Ringside
No Stop-over
What a Whopper
August *Teaching the Teacher*

	Spot Cash	
	Name the Day	
September	*The Jail Bird*	
	Late Lodgers	
October	*Gone to the Country*	
	Law and Order	
	Fifteen Minutes	
November	*On Location*	
	Hocus-Pocus	
	Penny-in-the-Slot	
	The Joy Rider	
December	*The Hustler*	
	Sink or Swim	
	Shake 'Em Up	
	Corner Pocket	

1922

January	*Lose No Time*	
	Call the Witness	
	Years to Come	
February	*Blow 'Em Up*	
	Stage Struck	William Watson
	Down and Out	Ralph Cedar
March	*Pardon Me*	Ralph Cedar
	The Bow Wows	Ralph Cedar
	Hot Off the Press	Ralph Cedar
April	*The Anvil Chorus*	Ralph Cedar
	Jump Your Job	Ralph Cedar
	Full O' Pep	
	Kill the Nerve	Ralph Cedar
May	*Days of Old*	
	Light Showers	
	Do Me a Favor	
	In the Movies	

June	*Punch the Clock*	William Beaudine
	Strictly Modern	William Beaudine
	Hale and Hearty	Al Santell
	Some Baby	Ralph Cedar
July	*The Dumb Bell*	
	Bed of Roses	
August	*The Stone Age*	
September	*365 Days* (the first of thirteen consecutive two-reelers)	
October	*The Old Sea Dog*	
November	*Hook, Line and Sinker*	
December	*Nearly Rich*	

1923

January	*Dig Up*	Craig Hutchison
February	*A Tough Winter*	
March	*Before the Public*	
April	*Where Am I?*	
	California or Bust	Craig Hutchison
May	*Sold at Auction*	
June	*The Courtship of Miles Sandwich*	
July	*Jack Frost*	
August	*The Mystery Man*	Hugh Fay
September	*The Walkout*	George Jeske
October	*It's a Gift*	Hugh Fay
November	*Dear Ol' Pal*	
December	*Join the Circus*	George Jeske
	Fully Insured	George Jeske
	It's a Boy	George Jeske

1924

January	*The Big Idea*	George Jeske
April	*Why Marry?*	Ward Hayes
	Get Busy	Ward Hayes

1925

March   *Are Husbands Human?*

1926

March	*Do Your Duty*	Ralph Cedar
April	*The Old Warhorse*	George Jeske
September	*The Doughboy*	(Produced by Snub Pollard
October	*The Yokel*	Comedies, directed by
November	*The Fire*	Jim Davis, and distrib-
December	*All Wet*	uted by Weiss Brothers
		Artclass in two reels
		each.)

1927

January	*The Bum's Rush*	Same as above

The Comedies of Larry Semon

Unless otherwise indicated, Semon directed his own films. They were released by Vitagraph through March, 1924, and were one reel in length until *Huns and Hyphens*, after which they were all double reels.

1917

August	*Boasts and Boldness*
	Worries and Wobbles
	Shells and Shivers
	Chumps and Chances
September	*Gall and Golf*
	Slips and Slackers
	Risks and Roughnecks
	Plans and Pajamas
October	*Plagues and Puppy Love*
	Sports and Splashes
	Toughluck and Tin Lizzies
November	*Rough Toughs and Rooftops*

| December | *Spooks and Spasms* |
| | *Noisy Naggers and Nosey Neighbors* |

1918

January	*Guns and Greasers*
February	*Babes and Boobs*
	Rooms and Rumors
March	*Meddlers and Moonshine*
	Stripes and Stumbles
April	*Rummies and Razors*
	Whistles and Windows
May	*Spies and Spills*
	Romans and Rascals
June	*Skids and Scalawags*
	Boodle and Bandits
July	*Hindoos and Hazards*
	Bathing Beauties and Big Boobs
August	*Dunces and Danger*
September	*Mutts and Motors*
	Huns and Hyphens
October	*Bears and Bad Men*
November	*Frauds and Frenzies*
December	*Humbus and Husbands*
	Pluck and Plotters

1919

January	*Traps and Tangles*
February	*Scamps and Scandals*
March	*Soapsuds and Sapheads*
April	*Well, I'll Be . . .*
May	*Passing the Buck*
June	*The Star Boarder*
July	*His Home Sweet Home*
August	*The Simple Life*
September	*Between the Acts*

October	*Dull Care*	
November	*Dew Drop Inn*	
December	*The Headwaiter*	

1920

January	*The Grocery Clerk*	
March	*The Fly Cop*	Directed by Semon, Norman Taurog, and Mort Peebles
May	*School Days*	Semon, Taurog, and Peebles
July	*Solid Concrete*	
September	*The Stagehand*	Beginning with this comedy, Semon shared direction with Norman Taurog through June, 1922
November	*The Suitor*	

1921

January	*The Sportsman*
March	*The Hick*
May	*The Rent Collector*
June	*The Bakery*
July	*The Fall Guy*
September	*The Bell Hop*

1922

January	*The Sawmill*	
March	*The Show*	
June	*A Pair of Kings*	
August	*Golf*	Directed by Semon and Tom Buckingham
September	*The Sleuth*	Semon and Buckingham
December	*The Counter Jumper*	

1923

January	*No Wedding Bells*

219

March	*The Barnyard*	
May	*Midnight Cabaret*	
August	*The Gown Shop*	
November	*Lightning Love*	Directed by Semon and James Davis
December	*Horseshoes*	Semon and Davis

1924

| March | *Trouble Brewing* | Semon and Davis |

The following Larry Semon shorts were made for Chadwick Productions and released through Educational. Each was two reels in length.

1924

| September | *Her Boy Friend* | Directed by Noel Smith |
| November | *Kid Speed* | Semon and Smith |

1925

| April | *The Dome Doctor* | |
| June | *The Cloudhopper* | |

1927

| October | *The Stuntman* | |
| December | *Oh What a Man* | |

1928

| January | *Dummies* | |
| February | *A Simple Sap* | Semon and Hampton Del Ruth |

Semon also made the following features:

1924

The Girl in the Limousine   Produced for Chadwick,
  (6 reels)   released by First
    National

1925

The Perfect Clown
  (6 reels)

The Wizard of Oz (7 reels)	Chadwick

1926
Stop, Look, and Listen	Pathé

1927
Spuds	Pathé

THE COMEDIES OF BEN TURPIN

Because Turpin appeared in numerous Essanay comedies for which he received no billing, it is improbable that his Essanay films can now be accurately catalogued.

For Vogue
1916

June	*When Papa Died*	The first six comedies were
	His Blowout (The Plumbler)	one reel in length and were directed by Jack
	The Delinquent Bridegroom	Dillon
	The Iron Mitt	
July	*Hired and Fired (The Leading Man)*	
	A Deep Sea Liar (The Landlubber)	
	For Ten Thousand Bucks	This and the remainder of
August	*Some Liars*	his Vogue comedies were
	The Stolen Booking	two reels in length.
September	*Doctoring a Leak (A Total Loss)*	They were directed by Rube Miller until his
October	*Poultry á la Mode (The Harem)*	contract expired in January, 1917.
	Ducking a Discord	
	He Did and He Didn't	

November	*Picture Pirates*	
December	*Shot in the Fracas*	
	Jealous Jolts	
	The Wicked City	

1917

January	*A Circus Cyclone*	
February	*The Musical Marvels*	This and the remainder
	The Butcher's Nightmare	of his Vogue comedies
March	*His Bogus Boast*	were directed by Robin
	(A Cheerful Liar)	Williamson
	A Studio Stampede	
April	*Frightened Flirts*	
	Why Ben Bolted	
	(He Looked Crooked)	
	Masked Mirth	
May	*Bucking the Tiger*	
	Caught in the End	

For Mack Sennett

In many of the Sennett comedies during 1917–18, Turpin made only brief appearances. These have been omitted in favor of those in which he starred or co-starred. Unless otherwise indicated, Turpin's films for Sennett were two reels in length.

		1917	*Directed by*
July	*A Clever Dummy*		
August	*Lost—a Cook*		
	A Pawnbroker's Heart		Edward Cline
October	*Roping Her Romeo*		Fred Fishback and
			Hampton Del Ruth
November	*Are Waitresses Safe?*		Victor Heerman
December	*Taming Target Center*		

		1918	
February	*Sheriff Nell's Tussle*		William Campbell

April	*Saucy Madeline*	F. Richard Jones
May	*The Battle Royal*	F. Richard Jones
June	*Two Tough Tenderfeet*	F. Richard Jones
August	*She Loved Him Plenty*	F. Richard Jones
December	*Hide and Seek, Detectives*	Edward Cline

1919

January	*Cupid's Day Off*	Edward Cline
February	*East Lynne with Variations*	Edward Cline
May	*When Love Is Blind*	Edward Cline
June	*No Mother to Guide Him*	Mal St. Clair and Erle Kenton
July	*Yankee Doodle in Berlin* (feature)	
August	*Uncle Tom without the Cabin*	Ray Hunt
September	*Sleuths*	F. Richard Jones
October	*Whose Little Wife Are You?*	Edward Cline
	Salome vs. Shenendoah	Erle Kenton and Ray Hunt

1920

January	*The Star Boarder*	James Davis
April	*Down on the Farm* (5 reels)	Erle Kenton and Ray Grey
June	*Married Life* (5 reels)	Erle Kenton

1921

February	*A Small Town Idol* (7 reels)	Erle Kenton
July	*Love's Outcast*	J. A. Waldron
November	*Love and Doughnuts*	Roy Del Ruth

1922

January	*Bright Eyes*	Roy Del Ruth

| April | *Step Forward* | F. Richard Jones |
| October | *Home Made Movies* | Ray Grey and Gus Mains |

1923

June	*The Shriek of Araby* (5 reels)	F. Richard Jones
July	*Where's My Wandering Boy Tonight?*	J. A. Waldron
September	*Pitfalls of a Big City*	J. A. Waldron
October	*Asleep at the Switch*	Roy Del Ruth
November	*The Daredevil*	Del Lord

1924

January	*Ten Dollars or Ten Days*	Del Lord
April	*The Hollywood Kid*	Del Lord
June	*Yukon Jake*	Del Lord
August	*Romeo and Juliet*	Reggie Morris and Harry Sweet
September	*Three Foolish Weeks*	Reggie Morris and Ed Kennedy
October	*The Reel Virginian*	Reggie Morris and Ed Kennedy

1925

January	*Wild Goose Chaser*	Lloyd Bacon
March	*Raspberry Romance*	Lloyd Bacon
April	*The Marriage Circus*	Reggie Morris and Ed Kennedy

1926

August	*When a Man's a Prince*	Edward Cline
September	*A Prodigal Bridegroom*	Lloyd Bacon
November	*A Harem Knight*	Gil Pratt
December	*A Blonde's Revenge*	Del Lord

1927

| January | *A Hollywood Hero* | Harry Edwards |

March	*The Jolly Jilter*	Edward Cline
April	*Broke in China*	
June	*Pride of Pikeville*	
August	*Love's Languid Lure*	
October	*Daddy Boy*	Harry Edwards

BIBLIOGRAPHY

Fowler, Gene. *Father Goose: The Story of Mack Sennett*. New York, Covici-Fried, 1934.

Franklin, Joe. *Classics of the Silent Screen*. New York, Citadel Press, 1959.

Huff, Theodore. *Charlie Chaplin*. New York, Henry Schuman, 1951.

Jacobs, Lewis. *Rise of the American Film*. New York, Harcourt, Brace and Co., 1939.

Keaton, Buster, and Charles Samuels. *My Wonderful World of Slapstick*. New York, Doubleday and Company, Inc., 1960.

Lloyd, Harold, and Wesley W. Stout. *An American Comedy*. New York, Longmans, Green and Co., 1928.

McCabe, John. *Mr. Laurel and Mr. Hardy*. New York, Doubleday and Company, Inc., 1961.

Montgomery, John. *Comedy Films*. London, George Allen and Unwin Ltd., 1954.

Payne, Robert. *The Great Charlie*. London, Andre Deutsch Ltd., 1952.

Ramsaye, Terry. *A Million and One Nights*. 2 vols. New York, Simon and Schuster, Inc., 1926.

Sennett, Mack, and Cameron Shipp. *King of Comedy*. New York, Doubleday and Company, Inc., 1954.

Smith, Albert E., and Phil Koury. *Two Reels and a Crank*. New York, Doubleday and Company, Inc., 1952.

Periodicals

8mm Collector	*Motography*
Exhibitor's Trade Review	*Moving Picture Weekly*
Film Daily	*The Moving Picture World*
Motion Picture News	*Universal Weekly*

INDEX OF NAMES

INDEX OF TITLES

237

The text for *World of Laughter* has been set on the Linotype in 11-point Caledonia, a distinguished type designed by the late W. A. Dwiggins, the eminent American graphic artist. The paper on which the book is printed bears the watermark of the University of Oklahoma Press and has an effective life of at least three hundred years.